THE BIBLE AS THE CHURCH'S BOOK

LIBRARY OF LIVING FAITH

John M. Mulder, General Editor

THE BIBLE
AS
THE CHURCH'S BOOK

BY

PHYLLIS A. BIRD

THE WESTMINSTER PRESS
PHILADELPHIA

BOOK DESIGN BY DOROTHY ALDEN SMITH

First edition

Published by The Westminster Press®
Philadelphia, Pennsylvania

PRINTED IN THE UNITED STATES OF AMERICA
9 8 7 6 5 4 3 2 1

Library of Congress Cataloging in Publication Data

Bird, Phyllis A. (Phyllis Ann), 1934–
    The Bible as the Church's book.

    (Library of living faith)
    Bibliography: p.
    1. Bible—Evidences, authority, etc.   2. Bible—Criticism, interpretation, etc.—History.   3. Bible—Study.   I. Title.   II. Series.
BS480.B498   220.6'1   82–7049
ISBN 0–664–24427–0   AACR2

CONTENTS

FOREWORD

The word "theology" comes from two Greek words—
theos ("God") and *logos* ("word" or "thought"). Theology
is simply words about God or thinking about God. But for
many Christians, theology is remote, abstract, baffling,
confusing, and boring. They turn it over to the profession-
als—the theologians—who can ponder and inquire into
the ways of God with the world.

This series, Library of Living Faith, is for those Christians who thought theology wasn't for them. It is a collection of ten books on crucial doctrines or issues in the Christian faith today. Each book attempts to show why our
theology—our thoughts about God—matters in what we
do and say as Christians. The series is an invitation to
readers to become theologians themselves—to reflect on
the Bible and on the history of the church and to find their
own ways of understanding the grace of God in Jesus
Christ.

The Library of Living Faith is in the tradition of another
series published by Westminster Press in the 1950s, the
Layman's Theological Library. This new collection of
volumes tries to serve the church in the challenges of the
closing decades of this century.

The ten books are based on the affirmation of the Letter
to the Ephesians (4:4–6): "There is one body and one

Spirit, just as you were called to the one hope that belongs
to your call, one Lord, one faith, one baptism, one God and
Father of us all, who is above all and through all and in all."
Each book addresses a particular theme as part of the
Christian faith as a whole; each book speaks to the church
as a whole. Theology is too important to be left only to the
theologians; it is the work and witness of the entire people
of God.

But, as Ephesians says, "grace was given to each of us
according to the measure of Christ's gift" (Eph. 4:7), and
the Library of Living Faith tries to demonstrate the diversity of theology in the church today. Differences, of course,
are not unique to American Christianity. One only needs
to look at the New Testament and the early church to see
how "the measure of Christ's gift" produced disagreement
and conflict as well as a rich variety of understandings of
Christian faith and discipleship. In the midst of the unity
of the faith, there has never been uniformity. The authors
in this series have their own points of view, and readers
may argue along the way with the authors' interpretations. But each book presents varying points of view and
shows what difference it makes to take a particular theological position. Sparks may fly, but the result, we hope,
will be a renewed vision of what it means to be a Christian
exhibiting in the world today a living faith.

These books are also intended to be a library—a set of
books that should be read together. Of course, not everything is included. As the Gospel of John puts it, "There are
also many other things which Jesus did; were every one of
them to be written I suppose that the world itself could not
contain the books that would be written" (John 21:25).
Readers should not be content to read just the volume on
Jesus Christ or on God or on the Holy Spirit and leave out
those on the church or on the Christian life or on Christianity's relationship with other faiths. For we are called to
one faith with many parts.

The volumes are also designed to be read by groups of people. Writing may be a lonely task, but the literature of the church was never intended for individuals alone. It is for the entire body of Christ. Through discussion and even debate, the outlines of a living faith can emerge.

Phyllis Bird is an ordained minister in the United Methodist Church and teaches Old Testament at Perkins School of Theology, Southern Methodist University. In this book, she stresses the central place which the Bible occupies in the life of the church and its worship. Using the theme of the pilgrimage, she points to the way in which the study of the Bible becomes a journey toward ever new and deeper understandings of the Christian faith. Her approach to the Bible is shaped by a lifetime of Christian nurture within the church, first as a Presbyterian in the Mormon ethos of Utah and then "returning" to the Methodist Church of her family. She acknowledges a particular debt to her father and his Bible class: "It was rich food for me, and it whetted my appetite. It is to my father, a lay teacher, that I am most deeply indebted for my love and knowledge of the Bible and my conviction of its revelance to contemporary life. I dedicate this book to him, who taught me by word and example to love the Bible with my whole heart and whole mind."

JOHN M. MULDER

Louisville Presbyterian Theological Seminary
Louisville, Kentucky

1

THE CHURCH'S BOOK

"Listen for the word of God!" With these words the reader
introduces the lessons from the Old and New Testaments
in the Presbyterian Service for the Lord's Day. Similar
expressions accompany the readings from Scripture in
other traditions. In modern Episcopal and Roman Catholic orders, and some Methodist practice, the reader concludes the lessons with the proclamation: "(This is) the
word of the Lord"—to which the congregation responds,
"Thanks be to God!" The choir in the Armenian Orthodox
liturgy heralds the reading of the Gospel with the words,
"God speaks." And in Protestant worship less governed by
liturgical prescription it is common to hear some reference to the reading of the Scripture as "God's holy word,"
often in an invocation. These various expressions, pre-
scribed by liturgical rule or dictated by practice, reveal a
common judgment about the Bible and a common expectation that explain its central place in the service of worship and in the life of the church.

Wherever Christians gather to worship, the Scriptures
are there, from the earliest orders of the primitive church
to the most recent forms of contemporary worship, from
the Roman Catholic Mass to the Protestant evangelistic
service. The word of Scripture may be reduced to set
passages or transformed into a litany, but it is rarely absent

altogether. And it is usually located at a strategic point in the service, leading into the confession of faith or the sermon, and surrounded by words and actions that draw special attention to it. The Scriptures are one of the few things that all Christians share, to which all have access, and to which all appeal—in some measure—as a source and norm for their faith. The use of the Scriptures in worship is evidence of the central and foundational role of the Bible in the church. That use in worship is also the means by which most Christians acquire their basic knowledge of the nature and content of the Bible.

The authority of Scripture, which the church universally acknowledges in confession and practice, has been expressed traditionally in the affirmation of the liturgy that it is, or conveys, the word of God. The meaning of that claim is the topic of this book. We shall examine the place of the Bible in the church and the church's understanding of its nature and authority, the origins and character of the writings recognized as Scripture, the criteria used in determining the compass of the canon (the authoritative collection of books; from a Greek word meaning "rule" or "standard"), and the means of interpretation that enabled the church through the ages to discern an ever new and relevant word in the ancient words. We shall attempt to show why the Bible has continued to be a source of life for Christians in every generation despite differing circumstances of life and differing understandings of the common text. And we shall investigate the causes and consequences of the battles that have raged in the church and rage once again over the interpretation and authority of the Bible. We begin with the church's practice, past and present, for the Bible is first and finally the church's book. But the ultimate and guiding question for each of us must be: What does the Bible mean for us today as contemporary American Christians? Tradition alone cannot compel our confession. We must make the church's affirmation our own through our own experience and reason. To enable that confession is the aim of this small book.

THE BIBLE IN WORSHIP

We began with a look at the standard Sunday service of worship. Whether it is a "service of the word" or a "service of word and sacrament," provision is made for the reading of Scripture. Protestant tradition has emphasized the centrality of the word and extended the reading by exposition, or proclamation. Both Luther and Calvin stressed the sermon as essential to the hearing of the word. Luther's comments concerning the service of worship illustrate that emphasis:

> Since the chief and greatest aim of any Service is to preach and teach God's Word, we have arranged for sermons and lessons as follows: For the holy day of Sunday we retain the customary Epistles and Gospels and have three sermons. Early at five or six o'clock a few psalms are chanted for Matins. A sermon follows on the Epistle of the day, chiefly for the sake of the servants, so that they, too, may be cared for and hear God's Word, if perchance they cannot be present at the other sermons. . . .
>
> At the Mass, at eight or nine o'clock, there is preaching on the Gospel appointed for the day. At Vespers in the afternoon there is preaching . . . on the Old Testament, taken in proper order. . . . This, we think, provides sufficient preaching and teaching for the layman; he who desires more, will find an abundance on the other days.

Calvin emphasized the inseparability of reading and explication of the word, treating them as a single element of the service. He also stressed the action of the Holy Spirit, enabling the words of the minister to be heard as God's own speaking.

But the Bible in worship is not confined to the lessons and homily. The entire service is framed in biblical language and transmits to every worshiper a significant, though limited, set of biblical expressions, ideas, and images. In the traditional services of both Catholic and Protestant worship, the opening sentences, call to worship, general confession, prayers, versicles (responsive verses), canticles (liturgical songs), and hymns, as well as the grace or benediction, were all taken directly from the Bible or composed of biblical phrases. Liturgical traditions preserve more of this biblical language, though its source is often unrecognized. But even those traditions of worship that stress spontaneity in prayer, personal witness, and freedom from set forms draw heavily upon biblical language and images. And newly composed liturgies often reach back to biblical themes and language as a major source, reclaiming a tradition neglected in the recent past.

While the selection of sentences, as well as translations, varies considerably among different traditions, most Protestant churchgoers will find the following familiar: "The LORD is in his holy temple: let all the earth keep silence before him"; "The hour cometh, and now is, when the true worshippers shall worship the Father in spirit and in truth"; "Let the words of my mouth, and the meditation of my heart, be acceptable in thy sight, O LORD, my strength, and my redeemer." But how many could find these quotations in the Bible? The first sentence is far more familiar than the book of Habakkuk, from which it is taken (Hab. 2:20). Although John is the favorite Gospel of many, not all will recognize it as the source of the second sentence (John 4:23). The third sentence comes from The Psalms, as did all of the opening sentences originally, in this case from the well-known Psalm 19 (v. 14).

These examples could be multiplied many times over, for the typical call to worship or opening word is still one or more sentences from Scripture. As we move through the service, each new act is accompanied by Scripture

sentences or is itself composed of biblical quotations or
allusions to Scripture. The versicles which originally
opened the service, and are preserved from the very earliest Christian worship, are taken from Ps. 51:15:

> O Lord, open thou our lips.
> *And our mouth shall show forth thy praise.*

The call to confession and the assurance of pardon were
traditionally given in scriptural sentences—e.g., "The
LORD is gracious and full of compassion, slow to anger, and
of great mercy" (Joel 2:13); "The saying is sure and worthy
of full acceptance, that Christ Jesus came into the world
to save sinners" (I Tim. 1:15); "If we confess our sins, God
who is faithful and just will forgive our sins and cleanse us
from all unrighteousness" (I John 1:9).

Scripture accompanies the offering in spoken sentences
and sung responses: "All things come of thee, O LORD, and
of thine own have we given thee" (I Chron. 29:14); "Remember the words of the Lord Jesus, how he said, 'It is
more blessed to give than to receive' " (Acts 20:35); "What
shall I render to the LORD for all his benefits to me? I will
offer the sacrifice of thanksgiving and call on the name of
the LORD" (Ps. 116:12–13). In some traditions, words of
Scripture are also spoken at the distribution of the Communion elements or in dismissing the Table: "I am the
bread of life. . . . Whoever eats of this bread will live for
ever" (John 6:48, 51); "Jesus said: I am the light of the
world; whoever follows me will not be walking in the dark,
but will have the light of life" (John 8:12). The service
commonly concludes with a grace or benediction taken
from Scripture: "The grace of the Lord Jesus Christ, and
the love of God, and the fellowship of the Holy Spirit, be
with you all" (II Cor. 13:14); "The LORD bless you, and
keep you; the LORD make his face shine upon you, and be
gracious unto you . . ." (Num. 6:24–26).

Most of these sentences "sound biblical" to us, even if we are unable to place them in their biblical contexts. But other parts of the worship service also present us with Scripture, though in even less recognizable form. The Prayer of General Confession in the Episcopal and Methodist tradition recalls many images from Scripture and is built up from biblical phrases: "Almighty and most merciful Father; We have erred and strayed from thy ways like lost sheep . . . ." Quotations from more than a dozen biblical books have been identified in it, including Isaiah, Psalms, I Peter, Proverbs, Jeremiah, II Chronicles, Nehemiah, Romans, I John, Titus, and three of the Gospels (Massey Shepherd, *The Oxford American Prayer Book Commentary*). But it is not only the traditional prayers that are derived from Scripture and call upon scriptural images and themes. Many modern prayers begin with a preface describing God's nature and work as known from Scripture. The following examples are from the Episcopal *Book of Common Prayer:* "Almighty God, who created us in your own image: Grant us grace fearlessly to contend against evil" (prayer for social justice; Gen. 1:26–27); "Almighty God our heavenly Father, you declare your glory and show forth your handiwork in the heavens and in the earth" (for vocation in daily work; Ps. 19:1); "Heavenly Father, whose blessed Son came not to be served but to serve" (for social service; Mark 10:45; Luke 22:27).

The Great Thanksgiving of the Communion service presents a synopsis of the biblical story of God's creation, guidance, and redemption. The new Presbyterian version begins as follows: "We thank you for commanding light out of darkness, for dividing the waters . . . , for creating the whole world and calling it good . . . , for making us in your image. . . . You have told us your purpose in commandments to Moses, and called for justice in the cry of the prophets."

THE BIBLE IN SONG

But Scripture is heard in our worship in yet more ways, as a word sung as well as spoken. The early church continued the Jewish use of the Psalter as its hymnbook, but composed new hymns of its own to be used alongside the old ones. Some of the earliest of these are found in the New Testament—e.g., the Magnificat (Luke 1:46–55) and the song of Simeon (Nunc Dimittis, Luke 2:29–32). Other new Christological hymns are preserved as nonscriptural canticles in the liturgy—e.g., the Gloria in Excelsis. But the tradition of employing the Old Testament psalms in Christian worship was never given up. They continued to frame our praise and our petitions in two ways, as unison or responsive readings or chants (the metrical psalms) and as the base and inspiration of much of our hymnody. While Calvin and Cranmer retained the Psalter for congregational singing (Calvin made fresh metrical translations from the original languages into the French of the people), Luther and the Wesleys composed new hymns that offered paraphrases and expositions of biblical texts set to popular tunes. The new compositions were musical homilies and meditations, which continued to employ the psalms but reached far beyond them, ranging widely over both Testaments. The hymns remained fundamentally biblical until the last century, constituting a kind of interpreted "people's Bible." English hymnals of the eighteenth century often printed the full biblical text at the head of the hymn which was based on it.

The legacy of this Reformation tradition of Bible commentary in song may be seen in any modern hymnbook, where the selection of texts and the variety of interpretations give a hint of changing theologies and changing approaches to the Bible over the past four hundred years.

Some examples from *The Methodist Hymnal* may serve as illustration. Fifty-two of the eighty-nine hymns based on Old Testament texts are from The Psalms. Among these are three versions of Psalm 103: "Praise to the Lord, the Almighty, the King of Creation" (seventeenth-century German); "Praise, My Soul, the King of Heaven" (early nineteenth century); and "O My Soul, Bless God the Father" (late nineteenth century). The most popular text is the Twenty-third Psalm, which accounts for four hymns, the earliest from the Scottish Psalter of 1650—"The Lord's My Shepherd, I'll Not Want"—and the others all nineteenth- and twentieth-century paraphrases: "The King of Love My Shepherd Is," "He Leadeth Me: O Blessed Thought," and "In Heavenly Love Abiding."

These hymns attest to the continuing popularity of the psalms in the hymnody. But New Testament texts and images also became popular sources, especially in nineteenth-century hymns, of which the following are examples: "Jesus Calls Us O'er the Tumult" (Matt. 4:18–22); "O Jesus, Thou Art Standing" (Rev. 3:20); "Make Me a Captive, Lord" (Eph. 3:1). New Testament texts are also the chief base of the hymns of Christmastide, Holy Week, and Communion. Yet the Old Testament provided the text for many a gospel hymn, though the connections may seem strange, and strained, to us. "A Charge to Keep I Have" (Lev. 8:35) was one of sixteen hymns composed by Charles Wesley on texts from Leviticus and published in 1762 in a two-volume collection containing 2,030 hymns on texts from Genesis to Revelation! Other eighteenth-century gospel hymns on Old Testament texts include "Sinners Turn: Why Will You Die?" (Ezek. 18:31–32); "Amazing Grace!" (I Chron. 17:16–17); and "How Sweet the Name of Jesus Sounds" (S. of Sol. 1:3). Use of Old Testament texts continued in the nineteenth century in compositions such as "Master Speak! Thy Servant Heareth" (I Sam. 3:1–10) and "We Are Climbing Jacob's Ladder" (Gen. 28:10–17), but the more recent compositions abandon the free Christological interpretation of the earlier hymns.

The fact that the connection between text and hymn appears strange and even unrecognizable in many of these examples is an indication that we no longer read and understand the Bible the same way our ancestors did. But the explicit attribution of so many hymns to biblical texts is also a reminder of the central place and formative power of the Scriptures in the life of the Christian church and especially in its worship. The hymns remind us too that the Scriptures played this role not simply, or even primarily, as a document from the past, but as a living word, evoking new responses and new interpretations from each generation. They show us how successive generations heard and appropriated the word, recasting it as they retold it.

The sermon has traditionally been viewed as the main element in Protestant worship, a legacy of Reformation emphasis on the word explicated and actualized as a present word of God calling hearers to a response of faith. But Protestant preaching has often lost or obscured the connection between the word of Scripture and the word of proclamation. Renewed ecumenical use of a common lectionary for preaching witnesses, however, to a revival of that Reformation emphasis in our time and attests a new unity of understanding and practice across a wide range of traditions, including the Roman Catholic.

THE BIBLE IN THEOLOGY

Our investigation into the place of the Bible in the church began with the central act of the church's life, its corporate worship, for the Scriptures are transmitted to us first and foremost through the service of worship. The use of the Bible in private and family devotions, in individual reading, and in group Bible study is an extension of this primary usage, interpreting and augmenting it through deeper personal knowledge and broader understanding. But the effective presence of Scripture in the church's life is not confined to worship and instruction. Scripture also informs and tests its deliberation concerning the content of faith and the demands of faith for life and action. In various ways and in varying degrees all churches appeal to the Bible as a primary source and standard for doctrine. Protestantism has traditionally emphasized the primacy of Scripture as a norm for faith, using the slogan of *sola scriptura* ("Scripture alone"). In fact, however, tradition plays a significant role in shaping all reading and use of Scripture, Protestant as well as Catholic, so that Scripture can never be wholly isolated as a norm.

Arguments concerning the authority of Scripture commonly focus on Scripture as a source and standard for doctrine, and attention is often further concentrated on a few central or disputed beliefs, such as predestination or the virgin birth. The actual *uses* of the Bible in formal theological argument and informal reasoning, in ethical judgments and spiritual formation, are typically disregarded in discussions of biblical authority. But it is in these uses that the living authority of the Bible is manifest. Some examples of this authority in use may be seen in the following situations.

1. There is in America today widespread concern over family instability and social disintegration. Many Christians have responded to this situation by calling for a return to biblical morality, finding a standard in New Testament models of family structure and family roles and in particular precepts and commands (e.g., Eph. 5:21 to 6:4; Rom. 13:1–7; Rom. 2:18–32). Others find authority for their critique and action in biblical demands for love, justice, and equality, applied to personal and social relationships (e.g., Mark 12:29–31; Micah 6:8; Gal. 3:28).

2. Peace has been an elusive dream in our world, but

among those who have chosen to live by that dream are
Christian pacifists and peace activists inspired by biblical
vision, blessing, and command (e.g., Isa. 2:4; Matt. 5:9; Ex.
20:13). Yet other Christians have regarded particular wars
as occasions of Christian duty, pointing to biblical understandings of war as divinely sanctioned means for combat-
ing intolerable threats to life, liberty, and faith (e.g., Deut.
20:1–4; Joel 3:9–10; Rom. 13:4).

3. Personal suffering and natural catastrophe drive us to
ask the meaning of life and its limits. At such times Christians turn to the Bible for understanding and consolation,
hearing there the voice of Job from his ash heap and the
voice of God from the whirlwind (Job 3:1ff.; 38:1ff.); the
psalmist's cry of dereliction and the psalmist's song of
praise (e.g., Ps. 22:1, 22); the reminder that we are dust
(Gen. 3:19); and the assurance of resurrection and death-
defying love (II Cor. 4:14; Rom. 8:31–39).

4. Movements for social justice and efforts to aid the
disenfranchised, the weak, and the poor have owed much
to the work of Christians motivated by biblical exhortation
and example: the prophets' cry for justice (e.g., Amos 5:24;
Isa. 1:17); Matthew's vision of the Last Judgment (Matt.
25:31–46); the Law's exhortation to remember the bondage of Egypt (e.g., Ex. 22:21; Deut. 15:15); and Jesus' relationship to the poor and outcast (Luke 4:18; Mark 2:15).
Plans differ and strategies conflict, but the biblical motive
remains.

Examples such as these may be multiplied and sharpened by reference to issues of current public debate: abor-
tion, taxes, environmental protection, the Equal Rights
Amendment, capital punishment, immigration policy,
homosexual rights, etc. In all of these debates appeal is
made sooner or later to the Bible, either directly or indirectly, in support of positions claiming the name Christian. The authority of the Bible for such issues is understood in different ways by different Christians, who make

different uses of the Scriptures and draw different conclusions. Some may be dismayed or cynical about this use of the Bible to support conflicting claims. What is important to recognize, however, is that all attempts to describe a Christian position, whether in politics or personal ethics, appeal ultimately, in some manner, to Scripture. How Christians use the Scriptures and what they expect of them will be considered in a subsequent chapter.

Our survey of the use and authority of the Bible in the church has broadened to include the political realm and narrowed to consider the realm of personal ethics and devotion. The Bible is found in all of the situations in which the church touches the lives of individuals and groups, from pastoral counseling to political action. But its use in the service of worship focuses and undergirds all other uses, reminding us that it is above all the book of a living community of faith, in which personal and corporate confessions are united, and intellectual and emotional needs are integrated. It is no accident that the Bible is most prominent in that service in which public worship and private need are most closely joined. The funeral service makes more extensive and more direct use of Scripture than any other service. In the time of loss and numbness and pain the words that speak most meaningfully are the words of assurance and the expressions of grief given to us in the Bible. Here we find the words we cannot speak on our own, the thoughts we dare not utter, and the hope which we are called to trust anew.

The Bible accompanies the Christian from birth to death, mediated by the church in its worship, its teaching, its counseling, and its action in the world. To be a Christian is to belong to a community whose identity and vocation have been deeply and decisively shaped by the Bible and whose present self-understanding and life before God and in the world continue to bear the stamp of its witness. That communal reality affects each of us individually as Christians. Whether we read the Bible or not, whether we believe it to be true and binding in all its parts or find it more or less irrelevant, incomprehensible, or abhorrent, we cannot escape or renounce its claim on us and still call ourselves Christians. The Bible stands at the center of that community in which we find our life as Christians. That is why the current battles over the meaning and authority of the Bible are so painful and the growing ignorance of the Scriptures so serious, for they strike at the root of our Christian identity.

2
CRISIS AND CANON

Contemporary Protestant and Catholic liturgies emphasize the special nature and authority of the Scriptures by identifying them with "the Word of God." Yet for many Christians today the meaning and force of that identification have become problematic. The church's public worship and proclamation are filled with the words and sentiments of Scripture. Yet there is throughout the church today a pervasive sense of loss of the Scriptures. In fact, the new liturgies and lectionaries, like the new Bible-based curricula, are themselves responses to this widespread recognition of loss. Behind these programs lies a serious, and continuing, crisis of meaning, authority, and use of the Bible, a crisis that finds expression in new caucuses and intradenominational battles, media wars, and church divisions and defections. It is a crisis that may be viewed as both a threat and an opportunity. In this chapter we shall examine more closely the signs and the roots of this distress.

SIGNS OF DISTRESS

Not all of the signs of crisis are clearly visible, and some that are may be misleading, masking deeper problems. Like a marriage under pressure, the lifelong union of the

24

church and the Scriptures is exhibiting various kinds of
stress and strain today. In some cases divorce has been
openly declared: the Scriptures' traditional authority for
faith and action is denied. In other cases a quiet separation
is in progress without public acknowledgment of disaffec-
tion. In still others the bond has been dissolved in reality,
but there has been no outward change: the Bible remains
in the pew—and on the best-seller list—but it is no longer
read or consulted as a source or norm for faith and faithful
action. Strain is indicated, however, not only by silence
and separation but also by loud protestations of faithful-
ness and excessive praise of the partner's perfection. Demands for unqualified belief of the Bible and assertions of
inerrancy are also signs of stress. Thus the signs are varied
in type and intensity, but in one way or another all declare
that the traditional marriage is in trouble or is, at least, at
a significant point of transition.

Let us listen to some of the complaints and defenses.
"I've tried to read it, but I just don't understand it." "It's
too hard." "It's boring." "It's full of laws that don't have
any relevance today." "I can't pronounce the names." "It
contradicts itself." "Everybody has different interpretations; how can I tell which is right?" "I expect the preacher
to know what it says and explain the important parts."
"Reading the Bible doesn't seem to make you a better
Christian." For many Christians who are neither hostile
nor defensive toward the Bible, it has simply become a
book that is not worth the effort to understand, a puzzle
or problem not worth solving. It neither excites nor com-
pels use. The relationship is maintained only through past
association, without present conviction.

For others, however, who also count themselves Christians, the Bible is not so much incomprehensible as incredible or offensive, at least in significant part. For them some
form of separation or divorce seems required, or some
other fundamental change in the relationship—or the

partner. "The Bible is full of miracles that are contrary to the understanding of modern science." "It contains a primitive morality and a repressive view of sexuality." "It proclaims a narrow view of salvation that excludes people of other faiths." "The Bible teaches the subordination of women." "It glorifies war and sanctifies slaughter in God's name." "It teaches the subjugation of nature and gives license to human destruction of the earth's resources."

And for still others, the problem with the Bible is seen primarily as a problem of the believer. If the relationship is difficult, they argue, it is because those who call themselves Christians lack commitment or have taken the wrong approach to the Scriptures. When we find the Bible meaningless or offensive, we are setting fallible human judgment over the infallible word of God. The fundamental problem is lack of faith and refusal to submit our minds and wills to the word of God. "The Bible is the inspired word of God and infallible in all its parts." "God cannot lie or contradict himself; therefore the Bible can contain no error or contradiction." "The Bible contains mysteries that our finite minds cannot comprehend." "The Holy Spirit gives right understanding to those who prayerfully search God's holy word." "The Scriptures contain God's plan for our lives."

These views are only a sample of current opinions and arguments, but they suggest something of the range and variety of contemporary understandings and expectations of Scripture. The variety is significant, for it is one index of the pluralism that characterizes the church today. Behind the various arguments and complaints lie a number of quite distinct, and sometimes conflicting, views of the nature of the Bible and of its relationship to Christian faith and life.

Some Christians view the Bible primarily as a source of ethical and moral norms and directives, guides to personal conduct, the ordering of family life and other relation-

ships, both individual and social. They seek God's purpose
and plan for their lives in the prescriptions, admonitions,
and examples of Scripture. Others regard the Bible primarily as a source of doctrine and seek from it statements
and standards of belief. For them the Bible is a book of
divinely revealed truths or inspired teaching about God
and the world and God's saving act in Jesus Christ. Still
others view the Bible as a book of prophecy and look to it
for the disclosure of God's plan for the world. They search
the Scriptures for signs of the course and consummation
of history and for the clues to the Final Judgment. For still
others the Bible is primarily a historical document. It may
be seen as a collection of ancient wisdom, whose insight
often surpasses the literalistic and utilitarian thought of
our modern technological age. Or it may be viewed as the
foundation documents of a dynamic faith, which has
moved beyond the understanding they preserve.

Contemporary Christian understanding of the Bible is
marked by diversity. But it also displays a substantial unity
of expectation. Most of the responses cited above assume,
in one way or another, that the Bible must *make sense* and
that it must *be relevant* to the lives of contemporary Christians. Where sense and relevance are lacking or uncertain,
the authority of the Bible is jeopardized. Authority
becomes hollow and formal without understanding and
the consent of reason. It remains at most simply historical.
But that is precisely the situation that threatens today. The
question that lies behind all of the complaints and defenses is the double question of meaning and authority.
How can the Bible have meaning for us today in a way that
maintains the church's traditional understanding of the
Scriptures as the "Word of God," but does not compromise
or coerce modern experience and reason? For many, the
problem of the Bible is understood as a conflict between
traditional interpretation and contemporary meaning or,
more simply, between the demands of tradition and rea-

son. In this situation, some choose to hold fast to the tradition and make reason conform or defer to its demands,
while others give priority to reason and experience, even
at the cost of breaking with tradition. In a later chapter we
will examine these two types of response and propose
another way of holding reason and tradition together. But
first we shall see how they came to be separated and opposed to each other.

THE EARLIEST CHRISTIAN SCRIPTURES

For most of the history of the Christian church, until
relatively recent times, the Bible was understood first and
foremost as a witness to Christ, and that witness was contained in both Old and New Testaments. The word of God
in Scripture was testimony to the living Word, made flesh
in Jesus Christ. As such it was a unity, characterized by a
common subject, God, and a common object, Christ. The
way in which this witness to Christ was understood differed considerably, but the fundamental notion of the
unity of the Scriptures was maintained.

The beginnings of this understanding of Scripture lie in
the early church and in the earliest witness of the apostles.
For these first Christians, who were Jewish in heritage and
hope, the Scriptures from which they sought divine guidance and illumination were the Scriptures of the syna-
gogue, the writings that constitute our Old Testament.
Jews and Christians of the first century A.D. shared a common Scripture, and it was this shared Scripture to which
the "Jesus party" turned for an understanding of the person and message of Jesus, and which it used in its debate
with the Pharisaic party and with other Jewish opponents.
The meaning and authority of Jesus as Christ (Messiah),
Lord, Son of Man, and Son of God was discovered in and
demonstrated by reference to the Jewish Scriptures,
which were referred to as "the Law and the Prophets,"

"the Law" or simply "the Scriptures" (literally, "sacred writings"). Even when the church expanded beyond its Jewish origins to include Gentiles, and even when the requirements of Jewish ritual law were set aside, the church continued to appeal to the Old Testament in its proofs and arguments, for the Jewish sacred writings were widely known in the ancient Mediterranean world and widely esteemed for their high spiritual and moral teaching.

So the Bible of the church from its earliest beginnings was the Old Testament, and the Old Testament alone, until well into the second century A.D. The Jewish Scriptures were simply accepted, without question or defense, as divine revelation. The Christian interpretation of those Scriptures, which found in them testimony to Christ, was not different in its method or presuppositions from Jewish interpretation of the time. Christians used the same typological and allegorical *exegesis* (a Greek term meaning "explanation" or "interpretation") as other contemporary interpreters to relate figures, words, and events of different periods and different compositions in a common pattern.

By the middle of the second century, however, the situation in which the Old Testament was the sole Scripture of the church had begun to change, and with dramatic speed and consequences it gave way completely by the close of the century. From that time on, the only canon recognized by orthodox Christianity was a two-part canon consisting of an Old and a New Testament. This rapid shift in the structure and content of the Christian Scriptures was the result of two distinct developments. It depended, in the first place, on the growth of a new body of distinctively Christian writings bearing the authority of the "Jesus tradition," that is, "the historical testimony to Jesus Christ and to what he signifies" (Hans von Campenhausen). But that alone was insufficient. The new two-part

canon came into being in response to a crisis in the interpretation and authority of the old Scriptures.

Christians in the Greco-Roman world readily accepted
the Old Testament as the sacred book that prophesied
Christ, but they also viewed it as a book of divine law.
According to the thinking of the day, this meant that the
Old Testament was viewed as something like "an ideal
manual of virtue, of religious duties, and of correct ideas
about God" (von Campenhausen). But the content of this
Jewish law, which claimed to be the perfect revelation of
God, appeared to be in sharp contrast to those aspects or
emphases of Christian teaching which were most appeal-
ing to Gentile Christians, namely, spiritual freedom and
inwardness. The Old Testament teachings seemed crude
and inferior by comparison. Consequently, when the
Gnostic theologian Marcion rejected the Old Testament as
the work of an inferior God, his program had widespread
and immediate appeal.

Gnostics (named from the Greek word *gnosis:* "knowledge") constituted a loose group within the early Christian
movement and also outside it. They were characterized by
a distinctive "spiritual" theology or philosophy that emphasized the perfection and transcendence of the true
God and the fallen state of nature and humanity. The
Gnostics viewed the visible creation with its imperfection
as the work of a lesser power. They believed that the true
self, or soul, of each person was imprisoned in creation by
the flesh but might be released through divinely given
"knowledge" and enabled to return to its true home in the
transcendent realm. While Gnosticism was eventually
repudiated by the church as heretical, some of the Gnostic
teachings closely resembled ideas found in writings accepted as orthodox—e.g., the identification of Christ with
the preexistent Word, or Wisdom, in the Gospel of John
and the idea of the soul's bondage to the flesh. But much
in the Gnostic world view was incompatible with Chris-

tian belief, especially the notion of intermediate divine
beings, to whom the Jewish Scriptures were attributed.

The Gnostic critique of the Old Testament threatened
both its unity and its authority as the revelation of God.
Some Gnostics found different levels of revelation in different parts of the Jewish Scriptures, assigning them to
different divine, or demonic, authors. But Marcion, in one
bold sweep, rejected the whole of the Old Testament and
set in its place a canon of purely Christian writings. His
aim in creating a Christian canon was to identify and en-
dorse a trustworthy body of writings within the growing
literature of the Jesus tradition. He sought for his canon
the most ancient and authentic witness to Christ, and he
found that first and foremost in the letters of Paul, whom
he regarded as the one true apostle of Christ. At the head
of his collection of ten Pauline letters he placed his own
"purified" version of the Gospel of Luke, which he understood to be the "gospel" referred to by Paul in his letters.

The consequences of Marcion's move were enormous,
and the reaction was swift. Marcion had destroyed the
only Scriptures that the church had ever known; but he
had also created the first Christian "Scriptures," that is, a
body of purely Christian writings with authority comparable to that of the canonical Jewish Scriptures. Orthodox
Christianity responded to this challenge by defending its
traditional Scriptures *and* by recognizing a new body of
Scriptures alongside it.

The church's first concern was to save its ancient Scriptures, to defend the Old Testament as the true revelation
of the one God and therefore authoritative as a whole. It
accomplished this by setting the Old Testament revelation
within a historical scheme of salvation. Thus it acknowl-
edged that parts of the law were no longer binding because they were framed specifically for the Jews and pertained to a particular era of salvation history, but it also
maintained an understanding of the law in its totality as

divine ordinance. The revelation contained in the law remained valid and was still essential to a true understanding of God's will and work as culminating in Jesus Christ. The law remained as God's eternal word in time, but now it was interpreted within a historical framework of prophecy and fulfillment.

This understanding of the Old Testament will probably not seem strange to us, but it may seem strange that such a view did not require a New Testament alongside the Old. In fact, the terms "Old Testament" and "New Testament" had not yet come into being, and until Marcion formed his Christian canon, no church possessed a generally recognized and closed collection of authoritative Christian writings. What the church placed alongside its Jewish Scriptures and what it appealed to in interpreting them was a living—and growing—Jesus tradition. This was passed on at first in oral form, in catechism, confession, and proclamation, but it soon began to be recorded in written Gospels, "memoirs of the apostles," as they were called because they were understood to contain the record of what the apostles had heard and seen. The "words of the Lord," sometimes referred to simply as "the Gospel," were read in public worship alongside the writings of the prophets, showing that they were regarded as having comparable authority. And the tradition to which the church appealed as authority for its belief was referred to as "the Law, the Prophets, and the Lord" or "the Sacred Scriptures and the Gospel of God." But the writings used in citing "the Gospel" varied from place to place and included many works not found in our canon.

There was a wide choice of Gospels, though Matthew seems to have been the most firmly established. The Gospel of Mark was little known, and John, which was popular among certain heretical groups, was ignored and even rejected by some orthodox theologians. At the end of the second century the Gospel of Peter was still being read—

with the approval of the Bishop of Antioch.

But the Gospels were not the only carriers of the Jesus tradition. Other writings were also read in public worship and cited as authoritative by theologians of the day in their defense and exposition of the faith. But here too there was neither uniformity nor limits. The letters of Paul were well known, but were regarded with suspicion by some major theologians. Alongside them, or in preference to them, we find letters of Ignatius, Clement, Soter, and Polycarp. And there were also the Acts of the martyrs and a long list of apocalypses, a kind of literature that contained predictions about the course of history and the end of the world, together with exhortations to repentance and teachings about heavenly things.

A NEW CANON

What caused the church to limit and define the essential core of this growing body of literature was the same need and interest that caused Marcion to create his canon, namely, the need to preserve and promote the earliest and most authentic witnesses to the gospel. It was a need to establish a standard, a normative collection of texts that would support the teaching of the church amid the confusion of new and conflicting traditions. The church did not begin anew in this effort; it took up the pattern and program of Marcion's work, correcting and extending his canon.

The basic pattern of Gospel and epistle was fixed by Marcion. And the principle of "apostolic" origin was already widely recognized as the norm for determining original and reliable tradition. The orthodox or catholic (meaning "general" or "universal") canon differed from Marcion's primarily in its understanding and application of that apostolic principle. Marcion recognized the authority of only one apostle, Paul, and reconstructed a "Pauline" Gospel to conform to his idea of the original gospel, a gospel that in his view had been perverted by the traditions of the church. The orthodox canon, in contrast, was more catholic or inclusive; it accepted the traditions of the church, but it sought to limit these to the most ancient and widely used. Thus it opted for a fourfold Gospel rather than a reconstructed "original" Gospel or a harmony of Gospels; and it extended the notion of apostolic teaching and authority to authors other than Paul or even the Twelve.

The church's response to Marcion established the core and the general contours of the New Testament canon, but its full extent would not be spelled out for another generation and its boundaries would not finally be fixed until the fourth century. Nor would the term "canon" be used of any Scriptures until that time. But the *idea* of a canon of authoritative writings was already established in the response to Marcion. And its essential content was determined by the end of the second century—in response to another heretical movement, Montanism.

Montanism (named for its founder Montanus) was an enthusiastic revival movement of a "New Prophecy" which spread rapidly through the church in the late second century. It emphasized the imminent return of Christ and the new gift of the Spirit, which it identified with the Paraclete promised in the Gospel of John. The Montanists stressed the new revelation given through their prophets and set forth their visions in new apocalypses. Where they departed most significantly from orthodox tradition was in their claim of superior authority for the New Prophecy of the Paraclete over the former revelation. They also disturbed the churches by the "strange" forms of their ecstasy, the role of women in their movement, and their embrace of martyrdom.

The catholic response to the threat of the new movement with its flood of new scriptures was to close the

canon by excluding all "new" writings, especially the
apocalypses, which appealed to the Spirit for their authority rather than the tradition of the apostolic teaching. The
response to the Montanists fixed and fortified the already
accepted principles of the developing New Testament
canon, namely the principles of historical witness (or "apostolic" origin) and general (catholic) use. It brought to an
end a period of canon expansion, in which the "memoirs
of the apostles" (the Gospels) had been extended to include the "other apostles" (Acts), and the corpus of epistles
had been expanded to include other "Pauline" letters (including the "pastoral" epistles—I and II Timothy and
Titus—and the disputed Epistle to the Hebrews) and also
the non-Pauline "catholic" epistles (James; I and II Peter;
I, II, and III John; and Jude). The expanded canon had also
opened its doors to a number of apocalypses. It is here that
the anti-Montanist reaction was most forceful. Of the sev-
eral Christian apocalypses widely used in the churches of
the second century, only one survived in the final canon,
the Apocalypse of John, or the book of Revelation.

From the third century onward the Christian Bible was
a two-part canon, whose parts were soon designated as
"Old Testament" and "New Testament." This ter-
minology made it possible for the first time to think of each
collection of writings as a whole, but it also united the
parts and defined the relationship between them. The two
collections of Scripture were to be understood as pertain-
ing to a succession of "covenants" (Greek *diatheke;* Latin
testamentum). The succession implies continuity but also
a reversal in the old order of authority. The church retained the Jewish Scriptures, but it altered their meaning
and authority in incorporating them into its new canon.
No longer was the Old Testament the primary scriptural
source of testimony concerning Christ. The new writings,
based on the apostolic witness, assumed that function and
status. Direct witness took precedence over indirect, and

new teaching over old. Yet one truth was proclaimed by all. The Old Testament was not discarded. It continued to be read in the churches of the second and third centuries as it had been read by the earliest Jewish Christians, namely, as prophesying and prefiguring Christ. But now Christ, as known through the testimony of the apostles recorded in the New Testament, interpreted the Old Testament rather than the Old Testament interpreting Christ. The center of authority within the canon had shifted; but the whole continued to be read and interpreted Christologically.

There are two important points to emphasize in the church's establishment of a Christian canon. First, the idea of an authoritative Scripture did not require the notion of a closed canon. In fact, the boundaries of the New Testament canon were not finally fixed until at least the fourth century, and there has never been a universally agreed upon Old Testament canon in the history of the church. Furthermore, changes in the notion of what books were authoritative or canonical were made as late as the fifteenth century A.D. Thus the canonical status of the writings was not determined by the writings themselves, but by the church's acceptance of them as authoritative for its faith. Second, the determination of which books would constitute the canon was not based primarily on the criterion of inspiration, since many writings were recognized as inspired. In fact, the New Testament canon was shaped in opposition to such emphasis. The early church distrusted the claim of inspiration, insisting that the authority of a writing be tested by the norm of apostolic witness. The appeal to divine inspiration as insuring the truth of Scripture relates primarily to the defense of an established canon, not to its creation.

We have seen how the early church preserved, selected, and defended the body of Scriptures which constitutes our Bible. We have also seen something of how it understood and interpreted this Scripture and how that understanding affected the final selection and shape of the canon. What was characteristic of early catholic exegesis was a unitary understanding of the Scriptures and a symbolic, or figurative, method of interpretation. That unitary and symbolic reading continued as the dominant mode of ecclesiastical interpretation for well over a thousand years and is still dominant in parts of the church today. Traditional interpretation did not deny the variety or the complexity of the biblical writings; it recognized that the Bible speaks with different voices and different messages. But behind and through them all, it insisted, one voice and one speaker could be discerned, with one message of salvation —the same God and the same gospel confessed and proclaimed by the church of its own day. Through divine inspiration diverse authors gave expression in diverse ways to a single truth. If that ultimate word was unclear from their particular messages, which often appeared to conflict or to deal with wholly unrelated matters, it was assumed that the true meaning was hidden within them. That is why they had to be understood symbolically or "spiritually" rather than literally.

In the next chapter we shall see how this traditional reading of the Scriptures broke down under the dual impact of a new historical and scientific consciousness and the Reformation insistence on the "plain" meaning of the text. We shall also survey the rise of modern critical interpretation of the Bible and reactions to it.

3

SOLA SCRIPTURA

Two centuries after the death of Christ the church possessed a collection of writings that it recognized as containing the essential and normative traditions concerning the Lord. These documents had a privileged place among the many Gospels and traditions of the Lord and among the many other writings recognized as inspired, for these alone were understood to contain the original, true, and tested witness to Christ. The canon was created then as a support and guarantor of the "apostolic" tradition which the church proclaimed. Scripture and doctrine (i.e., the church's normative teaching) were correlated; Scripture served the church's proclamation but was itself based upon it.

The new canon of Scripture was joined to an older one, forming a two-part canon, which has been the church's Scripture from the second century onward. Once this canon was established, however, its use and interpretation began to change. By the fourth or fifth century, the Scriptures no longer served primarily as proofs for the church's teachings or as weapons in the battle against false doctrine. Now the Scriptures stood on their own. The Bible was understood as a book containing the unique and final revelation of God, recorded for all time and entrusted to the church as the ever-present, ever-available word of

God. The task now was to comprehend that record of revelation in its marvelous fullness and mysterious complexity, to discover and interpret the divine self-disclosure in Scripture.

EXEGESIS IN THE EARLY CHURCH

In the last chapter we noted that the primary way of understanding the Scriptures in the early church involved a symbolic reading. That was in fact the dominant "theological" approach. But there existed alongside it, and often in combination with it, another, more "realistic" or "historical" reading, and these two approaches together characterized the long history of exegesis up to the modern period. The historical reading focused on the narrative and "historical" elements of Scripture: its chronological framework, its succession of history-like stories, its references to historical events, its attention to times and places, its genealogies and its prophecies. This approach saw in the Bible a comprehensive account of the history of the universe, set forth in a single chronological sequence from divine origin to divine consummation. The Scriptures, in this view, contain not only a record of the history of the world but also the revelation of its meaning and end in Jesus Christ and his reign. The Bible then is the story, or history, of God's purpose and plan for the redemption of the world, a story revealed to the eye of faith in the most diverse, and sometimes unlikely, words and events.

This historical reading of the Bible held the two Testaments together by a time line. It was a natural and realistic approach and, for the most part, it took the biblical accounts at their literal meaning, or "face value." But because it understood this history in terms of an underlying and unifying divine activity and plan, it also attempted to relate the figures and occurrences of different periods to each other by means of "typological" or figurative interpretation, that is, to understand earlier persons, proclamations, and events as "types" of later ones, prefiguring or foreshadowing their full manifestation or fulfillment in the New Testament. Thus the exodus was understood as a type of baptism and the "sacrifice" of Isaac (Genesis 23) as a type of the sacrifice of Christ.

But the historical reading of the Scriptures had other consequences for interpretation as well. Since the world presented in the Bible was understood to represent the one true world, created and ruled by God's design, readers looked to the Bible for interpretation of their own age and for an understanding of their place in God's history. They identified themselves with the figures in the biblical story. They saw themselves represented in the story of creation and "fall," which became their own story as well as the story of their first ancestors. Their world and their experience "made sense" only when it was incorporated into "the one real world detailed and made accessible by the biblical story" (Hans Frei).

The other principal way of interpreting the Scriptures was the allegorical or "spiritual" interpretation, which was popular in the early church and dominated the ecclesiastical exegesis of the Middle Ages. This approach sought the "higher," spiritual meaning behind the literal sense of the text. The method was developed by Greek scholars in the third century B.C. to interpret the classical writings of an earlier age, but it was soon adopted by Greek-speaking Jews to interpret their own Scriptures. Christian exegetes found it especially attractive, since they identified the divine word (Greek *logos*), or spirit, to which it appealed, with Christ, the preexistent *Logos* (Word) known from John's Gospel. This divine *Logos*, they believed, inspired the biblical writers through the Holy Spirit but also continued to work by leading the interpreter to true understanding, revealing the hidden meaning of the texts. The *Logos* theology, which was the basis of Christian allegori-

cal interpretation, emphasized the unity of the Scriptures
as the revelation of Christ, Word of God and Word incarnate, and the unity of the *Logos* activity in both inspiring
and interpreting the Scriptures. By the work of the one
Logos the differences within the Scriptures and the distance between the interpreter and the Scriptures were
overcome.

In its search for a higher meaning, the allegorical approach judges the text in its literal or surface meaning.
What appears to speak of commonplace events or seems
crude or vulgar, morally inferior, or historically question-
able cannot represent the true, or ultimate, meaning of
the text, according to this view, but must be a figure or
symbol of the true word. The literal meaning is not to be
discarded, for it represents the divine word in earthly and
profane dress, inviting the reader to ascend by means of
spiritual exegesis to a higher plane of meaning. Those who
read under the guidance of the *Logos* may be led by way
of the Scriptures to encounter God.

But how could one be sure of the knowledge obtained
in this way, especially since the Gnostics used the same
methods to claim truth for their speculative theories? Tertullian (ca. 200) argued that interpretation of Scripture
must be ruled by the faith and teaching of the church, the
living tradition of the apostles passed on and guaranteed
by the church's teachers and bishops. The true meaning of
Scripture must correspond, he insisted, to the belief of the
church, referred to as the "rule of faith." Scripture and
tradition were two forms of witness to one and the same
subject, the living Christ, and thus were bound together
in an indissoluble reciprocal relationship. But the key to
that dual testimony, according to Tertullian, was the
church's confession and teaching.

Tertullian's attempt to harness exegesis to the rule of
faith succeeded only in placing exegesis in the hands of the
teaching and ruling authority of the church; it did not

succeed in stemming the growing popularity of speculative interpretation. Two centuries later, Augustine (354–
430) set forth a theory of exegesis which emphasized the
spiritual meaning and which became the basis of interpretation until the Reformation. For Augustine, scriptural exegesis was a process of spiritual knowledge, in which the
condition of the interpreter was an essential factor. Holy
Scripture could be interpreted correctly only when the
expositor was guided by the norms of faith, hope, and love.
But this exegesis, whose goal was knowledge of the love of
Christ, also required accurate texts, a clear concept of the
canon as a whole, knowledge of the original languages,
and ability to distinguish between the literal and the
derived sense. Augustine's rule for making this crucial
determination was as follows:

> Whatever there is in the word of God that cannot, when
> taken literally, be referred either to purity of life or sound-
> ness of doctrine, you may set down as figurative. Purity of
> life has reference to the love of God and one's neighbor;
> soundness of doctrine to the knowledge of God and one's
> neighbor.

Thus the exercise which began with the literal text was
able by this method to escape its difficulties by shifting to
another level. It is no wonder this was a popular method,
for the literal text posed serious problems for ancient as
well as modern interpreters.

Medieval exegesis continued along the lines set out in
the early church, developing a "hermeneutical" theory, or
system of interpretation, which recognized four "senses,"
or layers of meaning, in the biblical text. The first was the
literal, or historical, and the second the *allegorical,* or
mystical. The third sense, called the *tropological,* referred
to the moral meaning of the text; while the fourth, the
analogical sense, revealed the eschatological meaning,
that is, the spiritual meaning as it pertained to future and

heavenly realities. With this fourfold approach every text was capable of yielding at least one "acceptable" meaning, and often many.

THE BIBLE IN THE REFORMATION

By the late Middle Ages this elaborate and esoteric system of interpretation had grown so rigid and topheavy and so bound to church dogma that it readily collapsed under the assault of the Reformation. Luther challenged a corrupt church with an appeal to Scripture as the norm of faith and doctrine. The Bible, as the original and universally accessible presentation of the gospel, was lifted up as the source of judgment and renewal. But for Luther and his Reformed colleagues it was the "plain" or literal meaning of the text, rather than the "spiritual" or allegorical sense, that was understood to convey the intention of its divine author. The literal reading, which Luther preferred to call "grammatical" or "historical," gave access, in his view, to the unique self-communication of God in the Scriptures, while the fanciful interpretations of the scholars served to confuse and obscure it, setting human invention in place of the divine word.

The Reformers' appeal to the Bible as the primary and unchanging source of the gospel and their understanding of Scripture as the self-interpreting word of God set Scripture for the first time over against the church and its teaching office, or at least alongside it, as an independent, and privileged, source of authority. Thus the Reformation reversed the two interpretive principles of the preceding age; it set the literal reading over the spiritual or allegorical reading, and the word of Scripture over the word of the church. In this fundamental shift of focus and emphasis the Reformers opened the way to a revolution in the understanding of the Bible and its place in the church; but the full scope and force of that revolution lay beyond them. Both Luther and Calvin remained in their understanding of Scripture closer to the long tradition that preceded them than to most later interpretation. While both rejected allegorical interpretation, they continued to read the Scriptures Christologically and to employ figuration and typology in their interpretation, especially of the Old Testament. They also continued to assume the coherence of Scripture and doctrine, though they shifted the emphasis to Scripture. It is that shift, however, which was all-important. It was the hallmark of the Reformation everywhere and it had far-reaching consequences.

One of the consequences of the Reformation insistence on the primacy of Scripture in its plain or historical sense was a new interest in the biblical text and in its original meaning and historical context, an interest that supported the rise of new linguistic and historical studies. Another consequence was a need for new ways of understanding disparities or conflicts in the content which could no longer be resolved by escape to a "higher" plane of meaning. Yet another consequence of the Reformation emphasis was a new concern for the hearing of the word and new attention to the link between exegesis and proclamation, a concern that had a profound effect on the shape and character of Protestant worship. These multiple effects worked themselves out over the succeeding centuries, but they were already evident in varying degrees in the work of the great Reformers.

Luther's insistence on Scripture alone *(sola scriptura)* as the norm of belief and practice rested on his conviction that Scripture was by itself "the most certain, most accessible, [and] most comprehensible authority," interpreting itself and judging all human words, including those of popes and scholars. It was the word of God spoken directly to its hearers for their salvation. And so that all might hear, Luther undertook to translate the Bible from the original languages into the German of his day.

But hearing and comprehension of that "most certain" word of God also required a new form of liturgy. Luther transformed the Mass by creating a new service of the word preceding the old service of sacrifice. It included the reading and exposition of biblical texts and the singing of new "spiritual songs" composed by German poets. Luther insisted on a sermon at every service to expound the text. That requirement should be kept in mind when his view of the "self-interpreting" word is recalled. Luther even proposed that the sermon be read from a prepared collection on the ground that "there are so few gifted preachers who are able to give a powerful and practical exposition of a whole . . . book of the Bible."

For Luther, the true content of the Scriptures was Christ, and not only of the New Testament, for he regarded the prophets and the law as the "swaddling clothes and manager in which He was wrapped and laid." Luther never gave systematic formulation to his understanding of the authority and inspiration of the Bible. While he regarded both the book and its authors as inspired and referred to the Scriptures as the "word of God," he never simply identified that word with the words of Scripture. Rather, the word of God was Christ, and those portions of Scripture which did not treat of Christ (or "urge" Christ) were not worthy of belief. Scripture's authority comes from the One to whom it bears witness, and it must be confirmed in the heart of the believer. Thus the authority of Scripture for Luther was both objective and subjective. And while the Bible was a divine instrument, it was also a human document—of decidedly uneven quality. Exegesis, according to Luther, must aim to discern the gospel, contained in both Testaments, and distinguish it from the law; it must also focus on what is clear and interpret what is obscure in its light. With these guiding principles, Luther boldly dismissed portions of Scripture as unworthy, including the books of Esther, II Maccabees, James, and

Revelation—yet he honored tradition by retaining them in his canon.

Calvin's understanding of Scripture was close to Luther's in many respects but was given more systematic and theoretical expression in his theological writing and commentaries. For Calvin, the key to the understanding and the authority of Scripture was the activity of the Holy Spirit speaking in Scripture but also prompting the heart and mind of the believer to recognition and assent. This "internal testimony of the Holy Spirit" is essential to the acknowledgment of Scripture as "the word of the Lord." For the words themselves are merely the record of God's speaking and are not themselves either inspired or authoritative. The content of Scripture, apprehended through the internal action of the Spirit, is the word of salvation, but the words of Scripture in their human and historical meaning constitute the essential and sole access to that divine word. Calvin's commentaries (which covered most of the Old and New Testaments) were devoted to clarifying the original and literal meanings of those words, as preparation for theological exegesis and proclamation.

Calvin's basic service of congregational worship stressed the word even more than Luther's and emphasized the act of preaching. His service of the word was meant to be joined to the Lord's Supper, providing a new service of word and sacrament in place of the Mass, which he wholly rejected. But the custom of infrequent Communion prevailed, leaving the new service of the word as the basic service. Calvin also introduced congregational singing into the service, but not the free compositions or paraphrases of Luther's German hymns. Calvin's congregations confined their musical offerings to the psalms in metrical translation, praying through them with the Holy Spirit in the Spirit's own words.

Calvin gave a more positive assessment than Luther to the full range of witness in the Scriptures and appears more of a "literalist." For Calvin the subject matter of Scripture was substantially identical with its literal narrative sense and was not sought in figures or in the opposition of law and gospel. Calvin associated the "law" with the Old Testament as a whole and hence with the promise fulfilled or ratified in the New Testament. For him, law and gospel belonged together, presenting in their union the story, and the offer, of salvation. And each was equally pervaded by God's word.

Both Luther and Calvin gave new emphasis to the authority of Scripture, drawing upon traditional views of the Bible as inspired and as "word of God" in their understanding of its authority. But both emphasized the continuing activity of the divine speaker and the necessity of encounter with that speaker in the heart of the believer, so that the authority of Scripture could not be located exclusively either in the words themselves or in the historical authors. Their views of the inspiration and authority of Scripture differed significantly from the rigid and mechanical views of later Protestant orthodoxy and modern fundamentalism. Neither had an explicit doctrine of Scripture. The formulations contained in the early Reformed confessions were a later development, associated with controversies of a later age.

Luther and Calvin transformed the place of the Bible in the church and the church's understanding of it, but they still belonged to an age in which the biblical world view and the contemporary world view could be held together as one and in which the true world was the world portrayed in the Bible and made accessible through a "literal" or "historical" reading. That unity, or coherence, of world views was fundamentally challenged in the succeeding age, and in our age is irreparably broken.

A New World

Beginning in the seventeenth century a series of inter-related revolutions took place in the way in which Western Europeans understood the world, revolutions associated with the rise of modern science, technology, and historical consciousness. These revolutions are still in progress, unevenly represented and appropriated in different parts of the globe and in different segments and strata of society. And their radical consequences are still only partially visible and partially comprehended. But one of these consequences is clear; none of us in America today lives in the same world as our biblical ancestors—or our denominational and confessional fathers, whether Luther or Calvin, the Wesleys or the Campbells. We take for granted what they could not even imagine. We have seen beyond the sun (which the biblical writers viewed as the boundary inspector of the universe, or a lamp hung in the dome of heaven), and we have walked upon the moon and sampled its sterile dust. We know of peoples beyond Eden and its world-encompassing streams, and we date life-bearing sediments in the rock of our still-evolving planet at ages biblical writers could not count. The Bible no longer encompasses the world as we know it, and to some it seems that the Bible can no longer interpret it either.

Disjunction between the world presented by the Bible and the world portrayed by modern science and judged by modern historical consciousness is the fundamental cause of the modern crisis of biblical interpretation and authority. The immediate cause, however, is commonly seen to lie in the rise of new methods of biblical interpretation, which appear to widen the gulf between the biblical world and our own and to attack, or at least undermine, traditional views of the uniqueness and unity of the Bible as the word of God. But the new way of reading the Bible, which

is described broadly as "historical-critical," is in fact a
product of and a response to that complex revolution
which produced the modern world. Its roots lie in two
sources of that movement, the Reformation and the Renaissance, streams which sometimes mingled, sometimes
flowed in separate courses, and sometimes met in turbu-
lent whirlpools. As an heir to both traditions, modern biblical criticism has struggled throughout its history with the
legacy of their uneasy union.

The new study and understanding of the Bible that
began to emerge during the Renaissance had ancient
roots, but new sources of knowledge and a new climate of
critical inquiry resulted in the rapid emergence of a whole
new body of knowledge and techniques of interpretation
that gained increasing acceptance, especially during the
eighteenth (the Enlightenment) and nineteenth centuries. Jewish tradition, followed by early Christian interpreters, had attributed the various biblical writings to re-
vered figures of the past, the earliest and strongest of these
attributions being the tradition of Moses' "authorship" of
the Pentateuch (the first five books of the Bible). That
tradition served to emphasize the special authority of this
earliest "canon" within the Old Testament Scriptures and
was widely accepted, though it lacked any support within
the Pentateuch itself. In fact, problems had been noted
with the attribution from the earliest periods of Jewish and
Christian interpretation. Some situations described in
these books seemed to date from after the time of Moses,
and the text itself contained contradictions and repetitions
that suggested more than one viewpoint or author. Similar
problems of internal contradiction and diversity were also
noted for individual books. But these remained isolated
problems that did not affect the overall understanding of
the Scriptures. As long as the Bible continued to be treated
as a whole, with emphasis placed on its divine authorship,
and as long as allegorical or typological reading was the

norm, the contradictions in the text could be dismissed or interpreted away and did not constitute a fundamental challenge.

What broke, or decisively challenged, the traditional ways of reading and reconciling the Scriptures was the new emphasis on the literal and historical meaning of the text, encouraged by both the Reformation and the Renaissance. The problems created by the new reading were further intensified by Reformation emphasis on the Scriptures alone as the source and norm of faith. Scripture became at once the keystone and the stumbling block of the new expression of faith. For translation of the Bible into the vernacular and the development of commentaries to aid exposition directed new attention to the original texts and their original meaning. And this exposed ever-new difficulties that had previously been concealed or considered inconsequential for faith.

The solution to the problems posed by the new historical reading of the Bible was found by a new class of biblical scholars in a more thorough and fully informed historical understanding. These scholars, trained in the humanistic sciences of the Renaissance and acquainted with a rediscovered Classical literature, analyzed the biblical writings in the same fashion as those other ancient writings, making internal and external comparisons of content, concepts, vocabulary, and style. The result of this comparative literary analysis was the recognition of a multiplicity of "documents" of differing dates, authorship, and perspectives within the collection of biblical books. This recognition of multiple sources and editions led to attempts to describe their order and origins and thus to create a history of the composition of the Bible, which could also be understood as a history of the religion of ancient Israel and of early Christianity.

The new historical-critical scholarship discovered a story behind the story told in the biblical narrative and read the narrative in the light of that reconstructed history. Thus the new approach resembled the old allegorical reading in finding the true meaning of the text, or the key to its meaning, in some reality behind the text—only it reflected the new spirit of the times by seeking a historical explanation rather than a spiritual one. For pious advocates of the new method, it was a means of liberating Scripture, and hence the gospel, from the shackles of tradition, freeing the word to be heard as its ancient authors had heard it, enabling readers to sit once more at Jesus' feet by the Galilean Sea. But for many, the new analysis had the effect of replacing a divine book with a collection of human writings whose revealing and saving power was far from evident. Scholarly interpreters might aim to free the word from dogmatic misinterpretation and allow the biblical authors to speak once again in their own voice and idiom, but the result for many readers was confusion of speech and the removal of the Bible to a distant and alien world. The radical move of the Reformers to place the Bible at the center of the church's faith and life and to restore the Bible to the people seemed to have the ultimate consequence of making the Bible an even stranger book than before and giving it over to a new class of esoteric interpreters, the new biblical critics—learned doctors who were often not even doctors of the church.

It might appear that the Reformation put the Bible into the hands of believers and the Enlightenment took it away. But that oversimplifies the situation. For the new criticism was the product of a new spirit and a new world view, one that could not finally be resisted or denied, though appropriation of it or accommodation to it varied widely over three centuries. The Bible could not be isolated from the new scrutiny, preserved in a world of its own, without ultimate loss of credibility and authority. For attempts to maintain the old views of the Bible in the new world betray recognition of the changed situation, and loss of the Bible's authority within it, just as much as direct denials of traditional claims. The fact is that the Bible no longer represents the world to us as it did to our ancestors. It no longer stands as a comprehensive account of world origins and world order, but is itself set now within a new and larger world, as one ancient document among others. The necessary consequence of that change is that the nature of the Bible's message and truth must be redefined, a demand which the church has viewed as both a promise and a threat. In the next chapter we shall examine the course of the new biblical criticism and the church's response to it. We shall also consider the consequences of that history for contemporary use and interpretation of the Bible in the church.

4

THE NEW CRITICISM

The Bible has been throughout the ages a primary source
of renewal in the church. It has offered to the church of
every age deep waters from which to drink and sustained
it through long droughts. But in our time the waters have
run dry for many and grown bitter for others. Those who
still drink from this spring are engaged in a heated battle
over territorial rights. For the church today is deeply di-
vided over interpretation of the Bible, and the conflict is
felt in the public arena as well as in church sessions.

In the last chapter we argued that the roots of the current crisis and conflict lie in a revolution in our understanding of the world that may be characterized broadly
as scientific and historical, and in the rise of new perspectives and new methods in biblical study, born of that new
understanding and sharing the same scientific (critical)
and historical orientation. While the beginnings of the
new world view lay in the sixteenth century, it was not
until the eighteenth century and the extension of the
scientific perspective to the realm of history that its impact on biblical study began to be felt and its implications
for traditional understanding of the Bible recognized.
Reactions to the new learning differed according to time
and temperament, but the initial response of the church
was generally to reject the new method and devise new

defenses for traditional views. This move had the effect of delaying acceptance and hardening resistance to the new learning, but this could not stop it altogether, nor could the church remain unaffected by it, even in opposition to it.

The scientific and historical perspective that character-ized eighteenth-century learning as a whole was extended to the Bible by Christian freethinkers—and Pietists. Both opposed the dogmatic interpretation of the past and the ecclesiastical control that went with it. They hoped through critical inquiry to uncover the truth of the biblical message by penetrating to the original words in their orig-inal form and intention. For some, the new criticism was the tool for unmasking religion and rejecting its supernat-ural claims by exposing the Bible's human character, its crudeness and fallibility. For others, however, the new study was seen as enabling fresh encounter with the divine word as originally spoken to the prophets and apostles and access to the true Jesus behind the often-conflicting Gos-pel accounts. For the first time since the apostolic age the original word of the gospel might be heard again, they believed. Both groups challenged, directly or indirectly, traditional understanding of the authorship, inspiration, and authority of the Bible. Where that understanding identified the word of Scripture itself as divine, the new criticism was perceived as a clear threat.

Resistance to the new learning took many forms, from reprimand of its advocates to excommunication, expulsion from teaching positions, and even execution. In 1697, an eighteen-year-old student was hanged in Edinburgh for his "wild" assertions that Ezra was the author of the Pen-tateuch and that Moses had learned magic in Egypt. But while the measures used to repress the new criticism were often extreme, the reasons for resistance were under-standable. Some criticism was indeed wild and destructive in its aim. And the stakes were high. Defenders of the

tradition believed that essential belief, even the very keystone of the faith, was under attack. Truth and its inherited formulation were seen as inseparable.

The threat may be understood both narrowly and
broadly. The critical spirit always exists in some degree of
tension with tradition, whether or not it openly attacks or
rejects traditional belief. Questioning seems antithetical to
faith, and reason may appear opposed to revelation. Emphasis on historical process and event focuses on the
human plane rather than the divine, and natural explanation appears to exclude supernatural agency, or "interven-
tion." Critical inquiry acknowledges no limits or re-
straints; it conforms to no standards but its own. No belief
is immune to its probing, and no "fact" outside the sphere
of its investigation. Who can control such inquiry—or
judge its claims to truth? To some it appeared uncontrolla-
ble, leading easily to misinterpretation and misuse. To
others it was the creation of the devil himself, decked out
in the seductive garments of divine wisdom.

Pietist scholars took up the historical study of the Bible
in the spirit of Luther, whose emphasis on the human and
historical nature of the gospel and the gospel record
helped to make the Bible accessible to all Christians. But
criticism, we have seen, is open-ended; it threatens what
is secure. And it produces strange companions. Believers
were ranged with humanist scholars of antiecclesiastical
and even atheistic bent. The embrace of the new criticism
by the Deists in England and its contribution to a radically
atheistic rationalism in France led to a reaction by the
alarmed heirs of the Reformation which gave rise to a new
Protestant orthodoxy. Their attempts to defend the positions of their founders resulted in statements and confessions that were often rigid and lacking in the historical
sense of the great Reformers. In the name of Scripture,
Scripture was once again subordinated to the ruling authority of the church.

The early and strong opposition of Protestant orthodoxy and Roman Catholicism to the new scholarship had the effect of branding it as secular and of forcing it into opposition to the church, or at least independence from the church. Thus the church contributed to the autonomy of biblical criticism, freeing it on the one hand from clerical supervision, but also severing its ties to the dogmatic tradition, which continued to dominate the liturgy as well as private devotion. Precritical, or anticritical, understanding of Scripture continued to be the norm for most clergy and laity long after critical study had been established in the university, and attempts to reopen the door of the church to the ostracized interpretation were hampered by its history of secular development. But acceptance was only delayed. By the end of the nineteenth century, historical-critical method had become the scholarly tool of most of European Protestantism, and where resistance continued, it cut across confessional lines rather than defining them. Only Roman Catholicism stood opposed, as a church, to the new scholarship. In America, however, the battle was just beginning.

THE GERMAN BREAKTHROUGH
AND THE ENGLISH DEBATE

General ecclesiastical resistance was first broken in Germany during the eighteenth and nineteenth centuries. There the universities with their freedom from church restraint provided the environment where the new exploration could take place. And there in the first half of the nineteenth century, critical study took a particularly radical form in investigation of the Gospels and attempts to recover the "true" picture of Jesus behind their colored and conflicting accounts. The new scholarship evoked resistance from the church, but was not broken by it. And its advocates were not Deist debunkers, but Christians whose critical work was an expression of deep personal piety.

Biblical criticism in Germany influenced theological discussion in both the church and the university, for the universities were the primary centers of theological debate and centers for the training of pastors. In the university, efforts to assimilate the new insights of biblical criticism gave rise to a new (or "scientific") theology alongside the new discipline of biblical studies (called "Bible science" in German). Thus the German breakthrough in the historical-critical approach to Scripture resulted in the development of two new disciplines. It also resulted in the dominance of German scholarship in both fields for most of the nineteenth and twentieth centuries.

England lagged behind the Continent in accepting a critical approach to the Bible, because of a number of factors. Among these were the closer relationship of church and state, which kept the universities under ecclesiastical control; the early Deist controversy (see below); and the Evangelical revival, which largely ignored the questions raised by the rationalist critique. The debate over the new criticism also took a different form in England than in Germany, one that significantly influenced the American debate. In Germany, discussion had focused on the problem of relating historical fact and religious truth, or *history* and *dogma*. German theologians turned their attention to the development of a science of interpretation (hermeneutics) that would enable movement from historical exegesis to contemporary faith within the framework of the church's traditional confession. The two approaches were not seen as mutually exclusive. In England, however, debate focused on the problem of science and faith, and more specifically on the conflict of *reason* and *revelation* as defined by early-eighteenth-century Deism.

The Deists argued that a fully rational universe, which

science demanded, excluded the possibility of revelation. The idea of a divine Creator and Designer was not excluded, but the notion of special divine action or communication in or through history was contrary, they insisted, to the laws of nature instituted by God. Revelation (identified with miracles) and prophecy had no place in the true world revealed by science. But if the possibility of revelation was denied, then the credibility of the biblical "reports" was challenged—and hence also the authority of the Bible.

The church won the first round of the debate, but the terms of the subsequent debate had been set. An overconfident young science embraced by critical religious thinkers forced the argument onto its ground. Defenders of Scripture were pressed into an uncritical stance and reacted by asserting the infallibility and the scientific credibility of the Bible in all its statements. As a result, biblical apologists attempted to give scientific proofs for the Genesis account of Creation, find evidence of the Deluge and Noah's ark, and defend the Bible's geography and chronology as well as its miracles. But in this defense the problems of literalism became ever more evident and the arguments more strained.

The event that occasioned the final battle and also cleared the way for general acceptance of historical-critical interpretation of the Bible was the publication in 1859 of Charles Darwin's *The Origin of Species.* Its effect was electric, for Christian orthodoxy had concentrated its efforts on the defense of biblical cosmology (theory of the origin of the universe), including a six-day creation in 4004 B.C. Scientists and religious skeptics acclaimed the new theory, but so too did numerous theologians who saw it as generally supporting current studies on the Pentateuch. For those who linked the authority of the Bible to literal infallibility, however, it was a battle cry. National debates took place featuring the scientific, religious, and political

luminaries of the day. And in 1864 some eleven thousand
clergy signed the Oxford Declaration, aimed at counter-
ing the new "heresy."

But three decades later the battle was over, except for
isolated pockets of resistance; biblical faith had made
peace with natural science through the mediating effort of
devout but critical biblical scholars. Two forces contributed to the truce and the terms of peace. (1) The scientific and philosophical community broadly supported Darwin's theory of evolution, which stood in direct conflict
with the literalist interpretation of the Bible. (2) A new
group of biblical scholars influenced by German criticism
was able to show that no real conflict existed between the
claims of science and the Bible.

The words of the Bible do not have to be defended as
infallible, these scholars argued, nor the biblical world
view forced to fit the categories of modern science.
Rather, the Bible must be treated on its own terms, as a
book of religious testimony, not a manual of science. The
Bible is the word of God, argued William Robertson Smith,
only as it contains the word of God. Infallibility belongs
primarily to the Word, and only secondarily to the human
record that enshrines it. With these arguments the Scottish Old Testament scholar succeeded, in 1881, in clearing
himself of heresy charges brought against his work. But
lingering distrust of critical scholarship by the church succeeded in depriving him of his teaching chair in Aber-
deen. Scotland was the last area of resistance in Britain. By
the end of the nineteenth century, critical biblical scholarship was widely accepted across the full spectrum of the
church in England, from Evangelicals to Anglo-Catholics.

AMERICA, THE LAST FRONTIER

In America, critical biblical study was a foreign import,
which did not finally take root until the end of the nine-

teenth century—though it was introduced almost a century earlier. During the late eighteenth and early nineteenth centuries, the liberal and conservative streams within New England Puritanism began to pull apart and confront each other. Both shared an understanding of the Bible as the final authority for Christian faith, but the liberals believed that conservative interpretation found its real authority in external creeds and dogmatic systems rather than the Scripture itself. They looked to the new criticism of the Bible as the tool for recovering and restoring the pure teachings of Jesus as the foundation of faith. The liberals understood the Scriptures as records of God's progressive revelation, culminating in Jesus Christ. Consequently they did not hold all parts of the Bible as equally authoritative, but emphasized the New Testament, and more particularly the words of Jesus and the apostles, as its essential core. They emphasized the human character of the Scriptures and the need for reason to determine the proper interpretation, insisting also that God's revelation in Scripture must be consonant with God's revelation in nature.

The liberals dominated Eastern Massachusetts and counted Harvard College as their intellectual center. Their opponents were a coalition of moderates and conservatives representing the evangelical and conservative Calvinist stream within Puritanism. They combined evangelistic fervor with a strong scholastic tradition and looked to Yale College for intellectual leadership. The conservatives were located primarily on the Western and Southern New England "frontier," but they had gained in strength as a result of the Great Awakening and in 1808 were ready to challenge the "Eastern establishment." They hoped to capture the Hollis Chair of Divinity at Harvard, which had become vacant in that year. When it went to a liberal, however, they responded by founding a theological school of their own and imposing a creedal

statement on its faculty to assure that it would not follow
Harvard's defection from orthodoxy. Andover Theological
Seminary was the first school of its kind in America, where
theological education was separated from other areas of
learning and placed directly under church control. The
new seminary was to provide the arsenal and equip the
troops for the conservative counterattack on the Harvard
liberals.

Since the conservatives had no biblical scholar, however, the new school finally called a Yale-trained pastor,
Moses Stuart, to prepare himself for the Bible chair. Stuart
began by studying the biblical languages and was soon
introduced to German biblical criticism, for which he developed great admiration, though his theology differed
widely from that of his German mentors. He accepted the
basic principles of critical investigation, seeking to understand the original meaning of the text and giving due
consideration to its various authors. But he was convinced
that this "grammaticohistorical" interpretation would ultimately vindicate traditional belief. Thus he attempted to
defend the inspiration and authority of the Old Testament, for which the liberals had little regard, by historical
arguments. But he was unable, in the end, to accept fully
or to master the new criticism (often called "higher criticism"), because of the suspicion of his colleagues and the
barrier of his own piety.

America's first experience with critical biblical interpretation was over by the middle of the nineteenth century,
dying without issue, it appeared, and without original contribution. The new study had been confined to a small
circle, and it had been a German import into a domestic
battlefield, a weapon for theological combat rather than a
rootstock for planting. Liberals, who had pioneered the
study, had no use for it in the end, for it was easier to seek
the single truth of reason and revelation through reasoned
intuition than textual study. Conservatives found it too

dangerous and never fully comprehended, or accepted, the aims of higher criticism. Biblical criticism had been a tool of religious programs, and in the middle decades of the nineteenth century, religion in America was characterized by new forms and a new spirit that had little place for scholarly inquiry and was often openly antagonistic to it.

In the early decades of the nineteenth century a new wave of revivalism swept the country and established itself on the frontier, giving rise to new denominations and sects and reshaping older ones. This movement, which bore the stamp of the frontier, determined the character and shape of American religion for the rest of the nineteenth century and much of the twentieth. It elevated emotion as the sign of authentic religion and emphasized individual decision and simple propositional faith. Reduction of the content of the faith to "simple gospel truths" led, however, to separation and sectarianism as different and conflicting interpretations were given of the "essential" content of faith. In the new religious wars the Bible figured once again, but this time it was at the center of dispute. Because of the Civil War, which drained and diverted American energies and intercepted intercourse with Europe, the battle over the Bible did not break in full force until the end of the century. When contact was again established with the intellectual world beyond America's shores, it brought in rapid succession two new waves of assault on the thought world of most Americans, challenging a far broader stratum of the population than ever before to come to terms with the scientific world view.

Darwin's writings on evolution had an impact in America similar to that in England, involving public debate by national leaders and immediate, scornful repudiation. His theory also gained rapid and widespread acceptance in the scientific community and among the more broadly educated segments of the population. It was in some sense

the idea of the century, and the idea that brought the final
passage from a prescientific world view to a critical scien-
tific-historical world view. The crisis this caused for traditional religious views was profound and prolonged, for the
religious regeneration that America had experienced in
the New Awakening had been linked to a theological retreat into a rigidly anticritical defense of traditional doctrines. But the widespread acceptance of the world view
represented by Darwin's evolutionary theory had also
made the old beliefs in their traditional formulation unac-
ceptable to many thinking Christians, who could no longer
integrate their intellectual and religious worlds. When
critical biblical interpretation was introduced once again
to American ground, it fell on prepared soil, took root, and
flourished. Its advance was marked by bitter resistance, by
heresy trials and church divisions, yet advance it did; and
this time it had come to stay.

THE FINAL BATTLE—OR WAS IT?

Biblical criticism again came from Germany, as a part of
a broad influx of German learning carried by American
students who had streamed to the universities of Europe
following the Civil War. By this time biblical studies had
become a mature and established discipline. Its radical
ideas had been tested and winnowed, and it was now possible to speak of "assured results" of scholarship. The fruit
was ripe for plucking, and the American scholars who had
savored it were eager to share it. Critical biblical study was
embraced and expounded by a new generation of American biblical scholars with evangelistic zeal—and conservatives rallied to meet them. Between the 1880s and the
1920s the battle raged with all the fierceness of a final
battle, and virtually every American denomination today
shows signs of that prolonged conflict. None was more
deeply torn than the Presbyterian Church, whose conflict

was symbolized in the heresy trial of Charles Briggs.

In 1881, the *Presbyterian Review*, taking note of the heresy trial of Robertson Smith in Scotland, began a series of articles on the critical study of the Bible, alternating between conservative and liberal positions. These articles served to inform a much wider public than ever before about the nature and purposes of historical criticism. They also produced a classic statement of the doctrine of scriptural inerrancy in the first article, coauthored by the Princeton theologian A. A. Hodge and the Allegheny New Testament professor Benjamin Warfield. The Scriptures, Hodge and Warfield argued, not only contain the word of God, they are the word of God. Hence all their elements and all their affirmations are absolutely errorless. Apparent inconsistencies and collisions with other sources of information are due to imperfect copies of the now-lost originals or failure to realize the point of view of the author. According to Hodge and Warfield:

> The historical faith of the Church has always been, that all the affirmations of Scripture of all kinds, whether of spiritual doctrine or duty, or of physical or historical fact, or of psychological or philosophical principle, are without any error, when the *ipsissima verba* [the very words] of the original autographs are ascertained and interpreted in their natural and intended sense.

The doctrine of inerrancy was strongly condemned by the liberal coeditor of the *Presbyterian Review*, Charles Briggs, on the occasion of his inauguration in 1891 to the chair of Biblical Theology at Union Theological Seminary. In his inaugural address he defended historical criticism, characterizing the dogma of inerrancy as an attempt to "prop up divine authority by human authority," which he condemned as "a sin against divine majesty." It was a barrier obstructing access to the Bible, thrown up out of fear that historical criticism would destroy its authority. But such errors as historians find cannot destroy the authority of Scripture, he argued, which is from God. Furthermore, he insisted, the claim of inerrancy is nowhere made by the Bible itself nor sanctioned by the creeds of the church.

In the uproar that followed, Briggs, in contrast to Robertson Smith, retained his chair—for the seminary severed its denominational ties. But he was suspended from the Presbyterian ministry on grounds of heresy. The Hodge and Warfield statement had been adopted as the official position of the Presbyterian Church, and it appeared that the "Princeton theology" had won the battle of the Bible —though it was already losing ground on other issues. But a half century later, biblical study at Princeton would be taught with the same critical assumptions and the same methodology as at Union and Harvard and Yale and Andover Newton. By the third decade of this century a critical approach to the Bible was the norm in the seminaries of all of the older denominations, if not in the pew. And in the middle of the century the Roman Catholic Church, the only Western church that had officially condemned historical-critical study of the Bible, opened its doors to it and commended it as a pastoral tool. Today, Catholics are among its most enthusiastic practitioners and advocates. And within conservative Protestantism, New Evangelicals are cautiously appropriating its methods and perspective.

Rejection of the new criticism was an attempt to save the "historic faith of the church" in the terms in which it had been delivered in a prescientific age. But a new age required a new appropriation of the historic faith that took account of the differences between the ancient and modern (thought) worlds. Defenders of an inerrant Bible had attempted to justify the Bible's prescientific thought in scientific terms, making its thought conform to modern notions of time, causality, and historicity. Thus they judged the Bible by modern standards of thought. They also claimed for it a system of truth that the Bible itself did not claim. Historical critics, on the other hand, insisted on taking the Bible itself as norm; its ideas and expressions were to be understood first of all in its own terms, within the ancient thought world in which they had arisen. This shift in perspective from external to internal criteria entailed no loss of essential belief or authority, they maintained, but rather enhanced appreciation of the Scriptures and ability to identify with its ancient hearers. As modern believers came to recognize that the Bible's authority did not rest in the accuracy of its predictions or in the scientific validity or verifiability of its story, but in the encounter with the living God to which its testimony was directed, they ceased to resist the new approach and welcomed it with relief.

Yet today once again arguments for inerrancy are heard in the land, and they are linked, as before, to an appeal to the Bible as the source and standard of morality and truth. In a world that seems to be falling apart, lacking a sense of values, direction, or purpose, many look to the Bible as the key to a restoration of faith and of order, a return to old ways and old beliefs. They find the cause of our moral confusion and social decay in the loss of a divine standard and the loss of belief in God's sovereignty and judgment. And they identify that loss with loss of biblical knowledge and authority, attributed to a liberal or historical-critical approach to the Bible which, they believe, treats it as a merely human book rather than as divine revelation and law. Only an understanding of the Bible as the inerrant and infallible word of God can guarantee its authority for faith and practice, they insist, and ensure against relativizing interpretation and indifferent use. In the next chapter we shall examine that claim and propose an alternative understanding.

5

INCARNATE WORD

The response to the reading of the Scriptures in the Catholic and Episcopal liturgy has the ring of tradition:

This is the word of the Lord.
Thanks be to God.

Yet it is actually a new element in the vernacular Mass and the latest Episcopal prayer book, without antecedent in the older liturgies, Catholic or Anglican, Orthodox, Lutheran, or Reformed. It is a new element of the contemporary liturgy—but not a new idea. The church has always understood the Scriptures as a unique and privileged locus of divine communication and has commonly referred to the Bible as the "word of God." But this traditional understanding was not previously a matter of public affirmation or assertion in the service of worship. The new declaration incorporated into the liturgy is a reflection of the new situation in which the Bible is being read and used in the church today. It signals a new prominence of the Bible in worship, or at least a new emphasis on the word; a new assertion of the divine nature of the word presented by the Scriptures; and a new recognition of the whole of Scripture as the word of God, for the response accompanies the readings from the Old Testament and the epistle as well as the Gospel (though the liturgy of the Eucharist distinguishes the Gospel by the more specific declaration, "This is the Gospel of the Lord").

The new response to the lessons and the new attention to the lectionary in preaching have a counterpart in a new emphasis on the Bible in the church school curricula and educational materials of all major denominations today. Behind the current emphasis on the Bible in worship and education lies a widespread recognition of a loss of the Bible within the church, a loss both of knowledge and authority. We saw in an earlier chapter that one of the results of the intellectual revolution that produced the modern world view was a displacement of the Bible from the position it had held throughout the pre-Enlightenment history of the West. The Bible in the new age no longer encompassed the world as it had for our ancestors. Its value as a source of religious, historical, and scientific truth was relativized, if not wholly rejected, and its unity was lost or jeopardized by new methods of interpretation. As a consequence, its authority within the church, as well as in the broader culture, was diminished. In an age of new and competing sources of knowledge and standards of truth, it no longer commanded general assent or respect. Public and private knowledge of the Bible lapsed, and it became a historical relic. And while the church continued to cherish its holy book, few knew in any breadth or detail what it contained or what it meant.

For many American Christians in the last quarter of the twentieth century, the perennial best seller has become an unknown book, as a recent Gallup survey dramatically illustrates: "Six in ten teen-agers are unable to name any of the four Gospels of the New Testament; four in ten teens who attend church cannot do so. . . . One-third of teens do not know the number of disciples Jesus had, while one in five among regular churchgoers flunks this question" (*The Christian Century,* May 13, 1981).

The loss, or at least the ignorance, demonstrated by

these findings is alarming, for not only does it mean a loss
of cultural heritage (evidenced in the inability of students
to recognize or understand biblical allusions in Shakes-
peare and other works of literature); for Christians, it
means a fundamental loss of identity. Lament is justified
and so are programs of restoration. But blame is often
misplaced, and many solutions fail to address the fundamental question of meaning that underlies the loss. For
the loss of the Bible has occurred as a part of a larger
cultural change and is not primarily the result of new
methods of interpretation or of deliberate attack upon the
Bible's authority. It is fundamentally a question of the
Bible's meaning, and hence credibility, in the modern
world. And since that is the case, the cure cannot be found
in a return to the understanding of Calvin or Luther or
Wesley, for we cannot restore their world, and use of their
language will not reproduce their thought. The Bible cannot again be understood as a history of the universe in the
way it was for earlier generations—and teaching "scientific" creationism will not restore that lost authority. Nor
can it become the determinative theological universe for
Christians simply by asserting its authority or memorizing
Bible facts. It can only be restored to effective authority
for Christians when it is both familiar and comprehended,
when it is read and heard in such a way that it provides
the determinative story and symbols and references for
Christian self-understanding, for worship, for theological
discourse, and for engagement with the world.

Liturgy and curriculum provide the structures to enable
that recovery, to assure familiarity and understanding. But
they cannot assure assent—which is the crucial element in
authority. Living authority, which transforms historical
witness into a contemporary claim, rests ultimately on
assent, an assent of mind and heart and will, and that is not
obtained by either nostalgia or threat. It is an act of internal appropriation and response, an inward act of reception

and submission that issues in an outward act of confession: "This is the word of the Lord!" In the traditional understanding of Reformed theology this action is made possible by the work of the Holy Spirit. Thus the authority of Scripture rests not in its words, nor in its inspired authors, but in the continuing activity of God in the writing, transmission, and reception of the word—even to the present hearing. And that divine activity is always characterized by human agency.

The temptation of the church has always been to assert the divine reality by denying or disparaging the human, and that is especially true in its understanding of authority. Authority belongs to the divine nature and hence, it is argued, to the supernatural, the miraculous, the transcendent. We emphasize distance, otherness, and immutability (changelessness) as characteristics of the divine and suggest that the authority of Scripture as divine word elevates it to a position beyond reason and doubt, where human faculties and frailties have no place. We think of Scripture as a source of timeless truth in timeless formulation and see modern thinking as its enemy. But the heart of the Christian message and the scandal of Christian faith point in exactly the opposite direction. God is truly known in the human, and God is most fully revealed in a particular human life—whose sign of authority was a cross. God is known to us through incarnation, as word made flesh.

That is the revelation at the heart of the Scriptures—and that is the way God is revealed in the Scriptures. The identification of the divine with the human at the center of the Christian faith must be our guide in approaching the Bible. It allows us—and requires us—to hear the "word of the Lord" in Scripture as a fully human word, marked by all of the particularity and limits of human experience and expression—a fully human word disclosing the divine Word. The affirmation of the liturgy is not a proposition concerning the nature or origin of the words, but a confes-

sional response upon hearing the word. The Presbyterian
formulation expresses it in anticipation rather than response, as an expectation, and obligation, of hearing: "Listen for the word of God!"

Learning to Listen

But how do we listen? How do we prepare ourselves to
hear the word of the Lord in the Scriptures? What do we
listen for? And how do we know that it is God's word that
we have heard? First, we must listen with expectation and
confidence, trusting the assurance of those who have gone
before us and those who surround us that God does indeed
speak through these words. That is the testimony of every
generation, and there is where we begin as we set out on
our own journey of exploration. Second, we must listen
with empathy, openness, and diligence. Accurate hearing
and understanding demands an effort of entering into the
experience of another. It is sharpened by a trained ear and
enriched by shared experience; and it requires a willing-
ness to set aside preconceptions and be led by the speaker.
Third, we must read with aids. Understanding the Bible
requires special knowledge and skill. The words through
which God speaks to us in Scripture are not our words;
they are not spoken in our language and they often concern matters unfamiliar or of little interest to us. We may
misunderstand the message or miss it altogether by failing
to understand its true subject or the intention of the
speaker. Hearing the word of God in Scripture requires
translation and interpretation. And fourth, we must test
what we have heard by our best reason, within the community of the church, guided by the church's tradition and
informed by personal experience.

We begin with the affirmation of tradition and of modern critical interpretation that the Bible is the word of God
in human words—more precisely, in human thought and

language. We encounter it as a fully human work, having no special language or logic of its own, existing in no special world of its own. Thus its message and meaning must be sought in the same ways and with the same tools as any other work of literature or written communication. This demands knowledge of the languages in which it is written, recognition of literary forms, sensitivity to changing moods and contexts, and attention to author and audience as well as occasion and purpose of writing.

The Bible is the word of God incarnate in a foreign land and language. The world in which its words were spoken is far from our own—distant in time and space and alien in culture. We need interpreters and guides to travel there, but we must make the journey if we are to hear with understanding. This journey is not different in kind from the journey we might make to Europe or Mexico or China —or from that which we must make to appreciate a work of foreign literature, even in translation. For understanding requires a movement into the world of the speaker. It also results in a new understanding of our own world and of the world to which we both belong. It is the journey into the biblical world that enables us to affirm the truth and relevance of its word for our own world.

The Bible insists by its form and content that the divine-human encounter takes place in time—particular, changing time. It may not be confined to a single time or place —not to biblical time and not to a point within that time —though the encounter in Christ illumines all others. The Bible is the record of myriad encounters, witnessing to God's character as an ever-present God initiating ever-new encounters. The word of God revealed in the Scriptures is not a timeless word, but a word spoken anew in every time—and hence in our time.

The Bible is the word of God entrusted to human minds and tongues, discerned by human hearts and intellect. Its expression is as varied as its speakers, its forms diverse, its voices many. Its viewpoints diverge and sometimes clash; its words take on new meanings as they are repeated by new speakers. The word of God in Scripture is not heard as a single voice and cannot be judged by a single model or measure. Sometimes it is heard as the roar of many waters and sometimes as the faintest whisper, sometimes as a shout of joy and sometimes as a wail of mourning, sometimes as sublime poetry and sometimes as deadening prose. Its speech is more conversation than chorus, more dialogue than declaration. But those who listen carefully to its many voices discern a single speaker and subject behind them all.

OUR STORY / GOD'S STORY

The Bible is a story with a thousand actors, told in dramatic form but in often-jumbled scenes, a very human story. It includes narrative and song, historical report and prophetic vision. It features soliloquies, choruses and voices from offstage, armies and fireworks and dance interludes. And in this drama, which was produced again and again with constant changes and expansion before reaching its final form, the line between actors and audience is removed and the audience is brought on stage. Such was the nature of its earliest reading or performance and such has been the nature of subsequent reading, as our hymnals testify.

"Were you there?" asks the spiritual in recalling the crucifixion, while other hymns give witness to participation in other acts and episodes of the biblical epic: "Come, O thou traveler unknown, whom still I hold, but cannot see"; "We have passed through the waters"; "On Jordan's stormy banks I stand"; "Angels we have heard on high."

The story the Scriptures tell is the story of our ancestors in the faith, and thus it is our story, for we are made members of this people through our baptism. The biblical story tells us who we are as Christians by disclosing our roots in Israel and the shoot sprung from Israel's stem. It is the story of an undistinguished people on the face of the earth, remembered only through their own record, a people whose sole claim to distinction is presented in the affirmation, "Once we were no people, but now we are God's people." It is the story of a sinful people, who failed to trust their experience of grace and exchanged their glory for an idol, who transformed the good news of liberation into the bondage of law, who betrayed their vision and crucified their prophets—our story—in two Testaments. But the Bible is also the story of God's grace meeting each new act of rebellion and distrust, a story of redeeming love that cannot be bound or destroyed. This story, which is always a human story, is also a story of divine presence and action. It is in rehearsing this story and entering into it that we learn to recognize the hand and the voice of God so that we may discern God's speaking and acting in our own time. The Bible, in its full and undiluted form, is essential to Christian faith, for faith is not a momentary affirmation but a way of life, and it is the Bible above all which shows us the meaning and manner of life as God's people. It reminds us that God's word is manifest within a world "contaminated" by politics and self-interest and ignorance—our world—and that this world which denies God is created and claimed by God.

We have characterized the Bible as story, though its literary form is complex and its contents diverse. Only a story can contain such diversity and movement and draw it together into a whole. We have described it as Israel's story, the story of ancient Israel and one of its heirs. But it is also God's story, for God is revealed in it as the chief actor, who onstage or offstage holds together all of its diverse acts and scenes. When we begin, however, with the notion that the Bible is a book about God or from God, we are tempted to dismiss as unessential the setting in which the story is located and lived. But that human historical context is essential to the story and to the revelation which it contains, and it is the point of contact with our own experience. God is not known in the Bible apart from human history, and more particularly Israel's history. The starting point of biblical faith is a community's experience and not speculative reason, nor a word "from beyond." Reason is an essential element of the biblical witness, shaping and testing its reflection upon experience, but the experience is primary, and it is first of all the experience of a community.

A QUESTION OF IDENTITY

The starting point of biblical faith and the center of the biblical story, as expressed in both Testaments, is an experience of redemption that issues in a declaration or confession:

> We were Pharaoh's slaves in Egypt, and the LORD brought us out . . . with a mighty hand. (Deut. 6:21)

> Once you were no people but now you are God's people. (I Peter 2:10)

That experience of new life, which is also an experience of a new identity, is the starting point of the Bible's theological reflection. The whole of the biblical literature may be understood as reflection on the meaning and consequences of that primary experience. It starts from the fundamental question of identity and extends to encompass the universe: Who am I, or who are we as a people, that we have been delivered, created? Who are we among the nations? Who is the God that has delivered us and given us life? What is the nature and name of this Deliverer? What does the Lord require of us? To what and for what has God called us? What manner of life befits a people called by the Lord's name? These are the questions that lie behind the Bible's collected writings.

The answers take many forms: narrative and command, parable and exhortation, prayer, song, myth, vision, sermon, statute, liturgy, letter. And they do not cease, for the questions are raised again and again in ever-new situations, from new perspectives, in response to new experiences. The old answers are reexamined, challenged, discarded, and reformulated, and new answers are given. So the Bible in its final form has the character of an extended dialogue, the ongoing internal dialogue of a community living in the presence of God and in the knowledge of God's hand upon it, a dialogue in which God is always a partner, whether identified as a speaker or not:

Who are we?

We are the children of Abraham, who followed God's call from a distant land (Gen. 12:1–9).

We are the descendants of Jacob, who tricked his father and cheated his brother and wrestled with the angel of God (Genesis 27; 32).

We are the abandoned offspring of mixed pagan parentage, whom God found naked in the wilderness and adopted and wed (Ezekiel 16).

We are a people dwelling in darkness, who have seen a great light (Isa. 9:2; Luke 1:79).

We are a light to the nations (Isa. 42:6).

We are children of God whom Abraham does not know and Israel does not acknowledge (Isa. 63:16).

We are a new creation, neither Jews nor Greeks but children of God through Christ and heirs of Abraham according to promise (II Cor. 5:17; Gal. 3:26–29).

And what is required of those who claim such an identity?

You shall love the Lord your God with all your heart . . . and your neighbor as yourself. (Matt. 22:37; Deut. 6:5; Lev. 19:18)

You shall not kill; you shall not commit adultery; you shall not steal. (Ex. 20:13–15)

You shall not wrong a stranger . . . , for you were strangers in the land of Egypt. (Ex. 22:21)

You shall be holy; for I the LORD your God am holy. (Lev. 19:2)

You shall not eat any flesh with the blood in it. You shall not practice augury or witchcraft. (Lev. 19:26)

And what does the LORD require of you but to do justice, and to love kindness, and to walk humbly with your God? (Micah 6:8)

Love your enemies and pray for those who persecute you. (Matt. 5:43)

Children, obey your parents. . . . Slaves, be obedient to those who are your earthly masters. (Eph. 6:1, 5)

And so the dialogue continues, led by the question of identity to the questions of vocation and duty—and ultimately to the question of the One who has moved us to ask the meaning of our life. That One, whether seen or unseen, is the true subject of the Bible's reflection. The answers we have cited are partial and, more significantly, they are out of context They are merely signposts of the ongoing dialogue within the community of faith, and they must be read and understood within that context. For while some of these answers address us today, others do not. The Bible does not present us with a series of propositions; its confession and assertions are embedded in a story, the story of a community, and each new generation of believers must encounter them there, by entering into that story and making it their own. The church's creeds and confessions and teaching attempt to lift out and lift up that which is essential to faith, and thus to provide a guide to our reading of the Scriptures arising out of the ongoing faith of the church, but they cannot substitute for the primary historical witness in all its rich variety and diversity of situations. It is only by moving into the story that we gain a sense both of its center and of its shifting scenes and are thus enabled to comprehend the new acts of the continuing drama being played out in our time. Those who have seen and experienced the works of God in company with the biblical people of God and have heard God's voice through their testimony will not seek God in that distant past nor limit the word of God to the ancient formulations. They will seek God in their own present, find God in their own experience, and confess God in their own language—or the God they confess will not be the biblical God.

We have characterized the Bible as the word of God made known through the conversation of a community about the meaning of its life as the people of God, a conversation that continues in our time in the continuing community of which we are members. Some implications of that understanding have already been suggested; others will be discussed in the following chapters; and many must be left unexplored. We conclude with one example.

The conversation we hear in the Bible is overheard speech. Its words are not directed to us, though we may hear them as personally addressed. Standing in the wings, we may find much that is said irrelevant to our situation, but we may also hear words that pierce our hearts and compel us onstage. Hearing does not depend solely on the intention of the speaker, but the speaker's intention must be respected. If we hear a word as spoken to us, it will be because we have found in the ancient context a counterpart of our own experience. But we must not assume at the outset that every word will find such resonance or that every word must be applied to us. We must be willing to remain outside the narrower circle of those more specifically addressed, while acknowledging our solidarity with them in the wider circle. Those in our time who are confined in prison will hear the Bible's words spoken to prisoners in a way the rest of us cannot. Few of us can properly claim the words of comfort spoken to the poor. They are not words addressed to everyone. But they are words addressed to the community of which we are members and the creation of which we are a part, and we may not withdraw ourselves from their impact. When our hearing, or overhearing, takes place within the larger community of a global church, we are helped to discover meaning and relevance in the biblical words without having to force them to fit our own limited experience.

6

"ABRAHAM BEGAT ISAAC"

"Abraham begat Isaac, and Isaac begat Jacob, and . . ."
Surely there is a better place to begin! How many people
have set out to read the Bible through and never made it
past the genealogies of Genesis—or simply skipped over
them? How many have embarked on a program of Bible-
reading and abandoned it in the description of the Taber-
nacle, the laws of Leviticus, or the strange visions of
Ezekiel or Revelation? How many who know and love the
Bible stories cannot find them, or find them full of baffling
details, when they turn to the Bible itself? How many have
sought bread, but found only a stone, indigestible and set
for stumbling—or a weapon to hurl at opponents? Why is
reading the Bible so hard, when we have been told it is
easy, that all we have to do is come to it in prayerful
expectancy and its doors will be opened to us? Is it because
our faith is too weak or our commitment too shallow? Both
are surely possible, but a major cause is false expectations.

THE BURDEN OF FALSE EXPECTATIONS

Protestants have created a set of expectations about the
Bible that invite frustration, dishonesty, and failure. We
have been led to believe that its message is simple, and
therefore simple for us to comprehend; that it needs no

interpreter; that in it the word of God is immediately
available to all who sincerely seek. And the burden on the
reader is increased by our emphasis on the Bible as the
sole or primary source of faith and on the believer as
interpreter. These expectations are further heightened by
the impressive evidence of church vitality and growth
associated with a Bible-centered faith.

Bible-reading and Bible-preaching have given new life
to dead churches and dead Christians. They have also
been instruments of an evangelistic and missionary movement that transformed a primarily Western church into a
global church, largely through lay activity. But the notion
that this effect was produced by the Bible itself, without
interpreters, is a myth. The Bible that has been presented
has generally been a highly selective and highly interpreted segment of Scripture, commonly the New Testament
alone, sometimes a single Gospel or selection of Bible passages. And it is typically accompanied by a series of questions or claims with Bible references as answers or proofs
—an extraction of truths similar to the traditional catechism. The Bible has been assigned a status in Protestant
legend that it cannot bear. It is not a self-interpreting book
in the simple sense we have come to believe, but is presented through preaching and teaching. It never stands
alone.

The Bible is always understood in the light of tradition
or of some doctrinal norm or presupposition, whether that
takes the form of official teaching (as in Roman Catholicism), confessional standards, creedal statement (such as
The Chicago Statement on Biblical Inerrancy), or simply
custom. And the creedal demands laid upon the Scriptures
by "Bible-believing" fundamentalists generally do greater
violence to the plain sense of the text than the demands
of liberals, who are often accused of revising or dismissing
the literal text. *Both* bring presuppositions and demands
to the text, however, presuppositions shaped by religious

and cultural norms. The main difference between liberal and conservative interpreters is in where they look for their norms of interpretation.

Conservatives look to tradition for their norm, finding it in a doctrine of inspiration, which modern interpretation has understood in terms of inerrancy and consistency. Thus conservative scholarship has directed its efforts toward explaining contradictions and problems in the text that appear to threaten the Bible's authority. Liberals, on the other hand, look to the biblical text itself for clues to its nature and meaning, seeking to derive norms of interpretation from this internal evidence. They see the Bible's diverse and conflicting statements as essential elements of its message and focus attention on the history of its thought and the dynamics of its witness. Both liberals and conservatives read the Bible selectively, however, giving attention to that which is most congenial to their own faith. Thus in reading the Bible, and in reading others' interpretations of the Bible, we must be alert to the ways in which theological—and cultural—presuppositions influence interpretation.

The simple, self-interpreting Bible that recent Protestant tradition has set before us is a myth and a mirage. It is also not the Christian Bible; for the two-part canon which the church claimed in its repudiation of Marcion has been quietly replaced in most contemporary usage by a single Testament—and a highly simplified version of that. The sad consequence of this is that in our amnesia we do not even recognize our loss. The real Bible, and the church's greatest treasure, is more complex and more difficult to read than this popular version—but far richer and more rewarding. The reward, however, comes only with discipline and guidance. We need not be ashamed to admit failure in our attempts, nor should we be intimidated by others' proclamations of success; but as long as we claim membership in the Christian church we must continue the effort of listening and of dialogue with this book in the full scope of its witness.

INTERPRETATION—BUT HOW?

The Bible requires interpretation—and this has always been the case since the time of the formation of the canon. The only question that remains is: What kind of interpretation, or whose interpretation? What approach is most helpful, most "true" to the text? Whose plan is best; and how can one judge whether the interpretation is right or wrong? So much seems to depend on getting the right interpretation. The question of choice is a serious one today, for we are confronted by many competing programs and plans of Bible study, like so many diet plans; and they make the same claim: your life and your health are at stake. In view of the many offerings and the "hard sell" accompanying some, it is well to keep a number of general principles in mind as guidelines.

First, we should expect Bible study and Bible understanding to be a lifelong process, and we should therefore be suspicious of "crash" courses—just as "crash" diets. Short, intensive courses can provide a valuable orientation to the substance and shape of the Bible, to its central message and themes and its main actors, but they are also heavily weighted with the particular views of the authors or leaders. Such programs must be supplemented by a more stable and varied diet, followed on a long-term basis; and that will include knowledge gained through the liturgy, preaching, regular group study of selected books and themes, private study and meditational use. Bible study is more a process of hearing and responding than the acquisition of a body of facts and propositions, a conversation rather than a collection of right answers. It is an ongoing dialogue with the biblical speakers, in which we bring our own questions, but in which we must also be willing to hear and ponder the questions and answers pressed upon us by the text. It may also be viewed as a journey over terrain in part well known, in part unknown. Each time we retrace a stretch we encounter new sights, discover new paths to lure and new wells to quench our thirst. When we set out on a journey of this kind, it is not so important where we start; it is more important to have a traveling companion. We can make mistakes—and we will. We can take time to rest and reflect. And as our knowledge of the terrain and the customs of the people grows, so will our confidence. We will not be afraid to leave the marked highway, but will feel free to venture out in new directions on our own.

Second, Bible study should be undertaken in the community of the church, and in the particular community of which we are members. If meaningful Bible study does not or cannot take place there, then there is something wrong with that community's claim to represent the church. This emphasis does not exclude individual or ecumenical Bible study, Bible study at one's place of work, or in schools and institutes. It is meant as a reminder, however, that understanding and interpretation of the Bible is a primary task of the church, one that should be integrally related to other forms and expressions of the church's work.

Bible study is a community work. But it must allow freedom for individual questions and decisions and time for uncertainty and doubt, just as it must seek the contribution of each individual. The teacher or evangelist who insists that we must believe the Bible in a particular way is really asking us to trust him or her, not the Bible. In the face of such pressures we do well to hold on to the Reformation tradition of the priesthood of all believers and to the idea of the Bible as the word of God available to all. Not all of us have equal training or insight, but all can contribute to the work of unfolding and appropriating the

Bible's message for the church today. We may read the Bible on our own and be transformed by it; we may "meet Christ" through the Bible where we lacked previous conviction of salvation; we may discover the gospel through the Bible without previous membership in the church. But if it is Christ that we have met and the Christian Bible that has been the agent of transformation, then we will be led into the community whose book this is to continue our journey of understanding in company with that community, that people.

Third, the understanding obtained through Bible study should be compatible with our knowledge and experience of God obtained from other sources—but not forced to conform to it completely. This means that what we learn from the Bible should not stand sharply against all that we have come through our life in the church to believe is true; its truth must be tested by the church's tradition, by experience and reason. But the Bible must also be allowed its own voice, to awaken senses deadened by the familiar, to press the church to reassess inherited views.

It also means that the knowledge obtained through the Bible may not be understood as a different order of knowledge, beyond human reason. Insofar as we understand at all, what is understood is human knowledge; and like all human knowledge it is a divine gift. But as human knowledge, it is always incomplete and corruptible. The truth we claim to find in the Bible can only stand as truth when it has been tested by our best reason and is in harmony with our total understanding. The demand for understanding does not do away with the realm of the incomprehensible or inexpressible, with the reality of mystery and limits. But it does mean that the effort to understand is not dissolved by encounter with the mystery of God, nor opposed to it. Silence may alternate with speech and inform speech, but the speech must make sense.

The reason that much of the Bible makes little sense to

us is that it expresses the thinking of people who understood the world in quite a different way than we do. Their
"strange" notions are not therefore irrational or illogical;
they are simply based on different presuppositions. They
make sense in their world, but not in ours. If it is believed
that illness is caused by demons, God's power to heal will
be presented as the casting out of demons. We do not have
to believe in demons to believe that God heals, or to believe that God has power over the powers that enslave us,
but we do need to know what demons represented for the
biblical writer in order to understand the point of biblical
accounts involving them. We set up barriers to belief and
understanding when we insist on reading our presuppositions into the biblical writers' expression and then find the
biblical statements "illogical," so that we must either reject them or create a special category of "divine" logic to
account for them.

One of the greatest barriers to understanding the Bible
is our willful or naive refusal to let it have its own word.
We are so fearful that its authority will be lost if we question it. We insist at the outset that it must agree in every
detail with the tradition handed to us, and so we labor to
make it say what we think it ought to mean. We think that
a book of revelation ought to reveal doctrines and propositions, and in our search for these we ignore the actual form
and content of the Scriptures and fail to recognize the
presence of the One who walks through its changing
scenes. Our search for words blinds us to hands breaking
bread. We press our expectations and demands upon the
Bible and then are disappointed when it does not yield
what we expect, or we create elaborate explanations to
produce the meaning we require. We insist on the precon-
dition of inerrancy or verbal inspiration or some other sign
to guarantee "truth." The tragedy of this situation is that
we exhaust our energies fighting the wrong battles, tear-

ing the church apart over false issues, while the world
hungers for the living word of God and the bread of life.

STUMBLING STONE OR SIGNPOST?
THE BIBLE'S GENEALOGIES

A clear eye and an honest mind will bring us very
shortly, in our reading of the Bible, to one of the prominent stones in the road through the Scriptures, namely the
genealogies (or "begats," from the verb used in the King
James Version). And whether it becomes a stone of stumbling or a signpost depends on whether we stop and read
it or pass on around it—as the lectionary does. The
genealogies should serve to alert us to the fact that when
we read the Bible we are traveling in a foreign land. For
they make no sense to us as theological expression (even
if lineages, and especially royal lineages, still have some
social meaning), and we cannot pronounce the names—
two clear reminders that we are not at home here. Our
understanding of a religious book, in which we expect to
hear the word of God, has no place for genealogies, or food
laws, or oaths and curses; and if we are honest, it has no
place for sacrifice either, though we have taken up the
language of covenant and sacrifice into our own theological vocabulary in such a way that we no longer recognize
their origins in practices of oath-making and ritual slaughter of animals. They do not belong to our cultural or religious experience, and so we eliminate them from our
reading or substitute our own meanings for them.

The genealogical lists are a reminder to us that the Bible
belongs to another world and that if we are to understand
it we must enter that world. We often behave in our biblical travels, however, like "typical" American tourists, who
want to enjoy a foreign country from the safe and comfort-
able distance of an air-conditioned bus or hotel, uncon-

taminated by contact with the local people except on our terms, in services and performances suited to our desires and expectations. We are like tourists who speak only English and reprimand those who do not understand us, who view the "natives" as children or mysterious folk of inscrutable minds. We want cheese in China and peanut butter in Paris. But then we are not unique in these demands, for our biblical ancestors longed for melons and garlic in the wilderness, despising the "awful" manna (—and we sing, "feasting on the manna"!).

If we really want to understand the Bible, we will have to get down off the air-conditioned bus and set out on our own, on foot, through the countryside and into the villages, along the city streets and into the marketplaces. We will stop and talk to the people we meet along the way, sleep in their tents and eat at their tables. We will carry a notebook for our own observations and questions (the most important thing), a small grammar and phrasebook to help us begin our conversation, and a guidebook written by someone who has lived in the land.

A good Bible guide, like any good traveler's guide, will supply background information about the time, place, and people, with road maps and plans showing the major roads and points of interest. It will include notes on the climate, terrain, history and culture, language and local customs. It will note and explain practices and ideas that are peculiar to the region and may be incomprehensible to an outsider. It should enrich the journey, not substitute for it. And it should be used critically. Writers of guidebooks have their own preferences and prejudices and blind spots. Readers must question their guides, and they must be willing to go their own way and to explore less-traveled roads. We may discover new vistas from little-used paths and note changes in the land and landmarks described by earlier travelers. The wells from which our ancestors drank may have dried up for us, but we may discover new springs bursting forth where others found only wilderness (as, e.g., in the new appreciation of the Wisdom literature which previous generations found sterile). Exploring the Bible is an ever-new experience no matter how many trips we have made, and it always yields new sights and insights.

This book is not a traveler's guide, but for some taste of what such a guide can provide let us look again at the stumbling stone set at the beginning of the chapter, the Bible's genealogies. What is for us an impediment, blocking the flow of the narrative, and a cause of consternation when we give closer attention to its details, is an essential feature of the Old Testament Scriptures and a link between the two Testaments. The first part of the book of Genesis is framed by an extended genealogy stretching from Adam to Abraham, while the book of Matthew begins with a genealogy running from Abraham to Jesus. Thus the two Testaments are linked through the structural device of parallel beginnings:

> This is the book of the generations of Adam. (Gen. 5:1)
>
> The book of the genealogy of Jesus Christ. (Matt. 1:1)

But they are also interlocked through the genealogy itself, for Matthew extends the Old Testament genealogy, so that the new story that he will relate is set within the structure of the old and interpreted as its goal or fulfillment. Matthew uses a common literary form of the Jewish Scriptures, rooted in the life and thought of ancient Israel and closely associated with Old Testament concepts of convenant and promise, to make a theological point. By introducing Jesus as the descendant of Abraham and David (Matt. 1:1), he places Jesus within the line of Old Testament messianic expectation (seed of David) and also presents him as the true heir of the promise to Abraham, father of the Jewish people and source of blessing for the nations. Thus Jesus is to be understood according to Mat-

thew's Gospel not only as the Messiah of the Jews but as
the one in whom God's promises to Abraham are fulfilled.

The theological purpose of Matthew's genealogy is
made clear by comparing it with the genealogy given by
Luke, which is strikingly different in detail, but equally
theological in intention. Luke has used different genealogical traditions to construct the line between David and
Jesus, so that both the names and the number of generations differ. The significant difference, however, is a theological one. Luke traces Jesus' descent from Adam and
God, rather than David and Abraham, and thereby em-
phasizes the universal nature of Jesus' mission, rather than
the fulfillment of specifically Jewish hopes and expectations. And by tracing Jesus' lineage from David through
Nathan, rather than Solomon (as in Matthew), Luke gives
further support to his picture of Jesus as a prophet. Thus
the two New Testament genealogies of Jesus are ways for
the authors to express their different theological interests
and indicate the different communities for which they
were writing. Although they use language that to us suggests biological claims, that is not their fundamental aim.
Genealogies, as used in the ancient Semitic world and in
many other non-Western cultures, function primarily as
social statements not as biological records.

The biblical genealogies use the model and the language
of biological descent to describe a great many different
kinds of connections between individuals and groups in
both time and space. They symbolize the existence and
persistence over time of various relationships, serving in
particular to explain and justify rights, claims, and obliga-
tions associated with those relationships. But as the relationships change, so do the genealogies, producing one of
the features that most baffles modern Western readers.
The same tribe or individual may be located in different
ways in different biblical genealogies; one line may be
grafted into another; originally alien clans, or even cities,

may be incorporated into a "tribe"; and generations may be omitted, collapsing the distance between the "original" ancestor and a later descendant.

The Old Testament contains many different kinds of genealogies with many different functions. Some examples include the great genealogical table of Genesis, which is split up into segments each having the identical heading, "These are the generations of . . ." (Gen. 2:4a; 5:1; 6:9; etc.); the "table of nations" (Genesis 10), which arranges all of the peoples and nations known to the ancient writer into three groups as descendants of Noah's three sons; the list of the twelve tribes of Israel, as sons of one father and four mothers (given in different versions in different sources); the census lists which count the Israelites by tribes, for military, religious, and tax purposes; the lists which describe the apportionment of the Promised Land by families (lineages) and tribes—and thus assure the place of each lineage in the heritage of Israel; the lists of priestly and Levitical families, establishing their rights of service at the sanctuary; and the genealogy of the Judean royal family, the lineage of David, which is extended by Matthew to become the genealogy of the Messiah.

The genealogies remind us that the biblical world is a man's world, for the genealogies are fundamentally lists of males, in which women do not normally appear. They highlight a broader social fact, that is, that the primary organizing structures of the society were based on an understanding of males as the representative and responsible figures. In such a society women literally "do not count," and that is so not only in Old Testament census lists, but also in New Testament traditions of numbering the population, as Matthew's account of the feeding of the "five thousand" makes clear. What the text actually says is, "Those who ate were about five thousand *men, besides* [literally, *"apart from"*] women and children" (Matt. 14:21).

The limited appearance of women in the biblical accounts as a whole is the direct consequence of this primary fact of a society organized around male roles (in both the Old and the New Testament), not the result of a deliberate denial of women's rights or value. That is not to deny the Bible's sexism, but to clarify its source and enable a better understanding of its signs and consequences. Most of what is recorded in the Bible pertains to the public sphere of political, religious, and military activity, and hence is the record of men's thoughts and actions, for that sphere is defined as the male sphere even when women participate in it. When we ignore the overwhelming male-centeredness of Old Testament and New Testament society, we misread the Bible's words, for we fail to recognize its silences and qualifications (e.g., by reading "five thousand [persons]" for "five thousand men") or the significance of those rare instances where women come to view and to voice. The Bible's sexism is pervasive; it characterizes both the structures and the thought of the society. But it is, for the most part, an unexamined legacy of the ancient Semitic and Hellenistic world, not a theologically reflective stance. It is deeply embedded in the Bible's language and the formulation of its message, but it is not the message.

The Bible's genealogies tell us of the importance of the family and of kinship organization in the social, political, religious, and economic life of Israel. They remind us that we organize society quite differently, treating individuals without regard to family ties and viewing vocation and marriage as matters of individual choice. The kinship structure of ancient Israel has left its mark not only on the social life and thought of the Bible but also on its theology, for a number of key theological terms and concepts have a kinship derivation. The term "redeemer" originally designated a near kinsman who was obligated by the kinship bond to uphold or restore the freedom, honor, property, or "name" (lineage) of a kinsman when these were threatened with extinction or alienation. When the great prophet of the exile calls Yahweh the "Redeemer" of Israel (Isa. 43:14, etc.), he uses the language of kinship to assure Israel that God will restore his own. The Old Testament laws address Israelites as members of a single extended family, prohibiting treatment of a "brother" as though he were a stranger. When the New Testament extends that duty of love to the stranger, it builds upon the sense of kinship that lies at the base of the Old Testament notion of obligation. It expands the notion of brother/neighbor; it does not negate it.

It is only when we understand the meaning and force of kinship ties based on male descent and the solidarity of a kinship community which underlies Old Testament thought that we can truly appreciate the radical words of John the Baptist to those who claimed descent from Abraham as a guarantee of divine favor: "God is able from these stones to raise up children to Abraham" (Matt. 4:9)! And only those who understand what it meant to be Jewish, male, and free will fully comprehend the declaration of Paul that these distinctions have no meaning in Christ, for kinship with Christ makes us *all* equally heirs of the promise and "sons" of Abraham and God. The language of "sonship," "inheritance," and "redemption" belongs to this complex of relationships and ideas rooted in the male kinship system represented by the biblical genealogies— a system that is fundamentally qualified and reinterpreted by Paul's words to the Galatians:

> In Christ Jesus you are all "sons" of God, through faith. For as many of you as were baptized into Christ have put on Christ. There is neither Jew nor Greek, there is neither slave nor free, there is neither male nor female; for you are all one in Christ Jesus. And if you are Christ's, then you are Abraham's offspring, heirs according to promise. (Gal. 3: 26–29)

7

THE STRANGER ON THE ROAD: HISTORICAL CRITICISM AND THE CHURCH'S FAITH

The church has traditionally understood the Scriptures as revealing Christ. But too often we seek a portrait and miss the presence, failing to recognize in our search the One who accompanies us on the road. In the preceding chapters we proposed the metaphors of conversation and journey as guiding metaphors for our approach to Scripture. These metaphors were suggested by the nature of the biblical material, which presents us with many voices in dialogue, the witness of a people journeying through history in conversation with God and about God. There are many ways of reading the Bible with profit and integrity. One of our "hang-ups" about the Bible is the idea that there is only one way, one right method, and one right message. And so we search for the key that will unlock the door, and we exhaust our energy in arguments over the right approach, when all the while the door stands open, inviting us to enter. What we shall find cannot be determined from the outside, not even from the reports of other travelers. Understanding requires personal experience. So we must finally step inside.

There are many ways of reading the Bible with profit and integrity. We can learn much from earlier, precritical understanding, especially from its holistic approach and its free association of ideas and images from different contexts. We can read the Bible symbolically and figuratively, allowing its images to play upon our minds and interact with other images, ancient and modern, to create new messages. We can meditate upon individual words and sayings, giving occasion to the Spirit to touch us and address us in our contemplation. We can sing and pray the psalms. And we can retell the stories, taking the various roles in turn: sitting in Pilate's chair; crying "Crucify him!" with the crowd; following Jesus, in the company of women, from Galilee to the tomb; conversing with the stranger on the road to Emmaus.

What we cannot do, however, if we are to read with integrity, is relegate the Bible to a special category of literature and logic in which our common norms of understanding and judgment are set aside as inapplicable. The historic Christian faith offers no support for a pious suspension of reason; rather, it demands of every age the best reason of which it is capable. Understanding of the Bible has changed over time—and not simply in recent times—because perceptions of the Bible and the biblical world have changed, and with them the questions addressed to the Bible.

Today the Bible is commonly perceived by Western Christians as an ancient historical writing, but it is also commonly read as a contemporary word, or at least as a word having contemporary meaning and relevance. Our problem is how to do justice to both views or claims without collapsing one into the other. The perception of the Bible as a product of the ancient world is shared by modern interpreters of all theological persuasions. All seek clues to the Bible's meaning in the past, in literary, artifactual, and other evidence from outside the Bible. All appeal in one way or another to archaeology. The difference between conservative and critical approaches lies in the way they use archaeology or other extrabiblical evidence.

Two Appeals to History

Conservative, or fundamentalist, interpreters typically look for data in ancient records that will confirm occurrences or events described in the Bible, especially those that appear strange or incredible to modern readers. They assume in their search for corroborating data that the biblical narrative represents the same kind of reporting of events found in modern historical writing and eyewitness accounts. Consequently, they seek wood from Noah's ark and geological evidence of a great flood, believing that such evidence will demonstrate the "truthfulness' of the biblical record, by which they understand its historicity. Historicity, or historical factuality, is seen as the key to the Bible's claim to truth and to the trustworthiness of all its statements. Conservatives appeal to external sources in an attempt to maintain the authority of the Bible, seeking "scientific" support for traditional views called into question by modern critical reading.

This kind of argument has had wide appeal—and not only among conservatives—because it appears to set faith on a rational basis and thus overcome the conflict felt to exist between modern scientific understanding and traditional biblical faith. It rests, however, on a misunderstanding of the nature of the biblical account and the nature of biblical authority. As a result, its defense is both unnecessary and a diversion of attention from the primary message of the Bible. It reduces the Bible to the category of historical information, conceived in modern terms and judged by modern criteria. An inevitable result is manipulation of the text to fit the interpreter's requirements of consistency and factuality, or retreat into the notion that the laws of nature as presently understood were divinely suspended or inoperative in biblical times. Such solutions do violence to the text and to the integrity of the modern thinker in their effort to defend the Bible's literal truth.

Historical-critical interpretation also begins with a literal reading of the text, which it insists on maintaining in all its contradictions. It turns to the records of the past primarily to comprehend the literary and linguistic features of the text, its thought forms and social milieu, rather than to verify its apparent historical content. It views the words of Scripture first of all as literature (whether originally written or oral) and hence as a form of communication within a particular sociohistorical context. And while that context may be extended through written transmission, the "original" context of speaking or writing always leaves its stamp upon it. Historical criticism attempts to reconstruct the original context (or contexts) of speaking and hearing so that the modern reader can "catch" the point and hear the emphasis. It aims to enable the modern reader to stand beside the ancient hearer and hear without being misled by modern expectations and demands foreign to the ancient speaker and audience. Historical-critical interpretation is a method, not a message; it is a way of approaching the text. And while it has been identified primarily with liberals, it is now employed increasingly by evangelicals.

The critical interpreter's first question of an account like that of the Deluge or the resurrection is not, Did it happen? or, How did it happen? or even, What happened? but, What kind of account is this? and, What was its meaning for its author and hearers? In the case of the Flood story, the interpreter asks, What was the meaning of the account in ancient Israel? Was it news, and if so, what was new? Why are there repetitions and conflicts in the account? and, What is its meaning within the larger biblical context? The answers to these questions are sought by studying the language, content, and forms of thought and expression found in other ancient literature from the biblical writer's world and in comparative literature of other peoples both ancient and modern. By studying recurring forms and ideas, critical scholars attempt to discern the fundamental issues and questions that lie behind the writings and give rise to them. They ask, for example, what purpose genealogies serve and what kinds of questions creation accounts answer. And they discover that what looks to us like history, presented as a sequence of acts or events, may actually represent a philosophical construct or social commentary rather than a report of past events.

THE FLOOD STORY: A CASE IN POINT

Historical criticism is a method, not a message, but use of it has generated a body of widely accepted results that forms the basis for continuing investigation and debate. In the remaining pages we shall examine a few of the ways in which this study has enabled us to achieve a richer and clearer understanding of the Scriptures and removed traditional obstacles. We began with the Flood story and conservative attempts to "document" its occurrence and its age. Historical criticism insists that we take the author's intention seriously and that we read the text first of all in the light of its ancient Near Eastern, and canonical, context. When we do that, we recognize that the author is not describing a historical flood in the life of our planet. Rather, the author is using the model of a catastrophic flood, experienced in numerous historical occurrences, to depict the undoing of creation itself, the annihilation by the Creator of all that had been created, with the exception of a specimen pair of each creature. That basic image of a flood, rooted in recurring historical experience, is elaborated in two different ways in the two versions that have been interwoven in the preserved account. One sticks close to the original flood metaphor and describes the blotting out or wiping away of life from upon the surface of the earth. The other links the Deluge to the account in Gen. 1:6–9 of creaticn by the separation of the primeval waters and consequently describes the destruction as an opening of the floodgates holding back the waters above and below the earth and a return of the primeval chaos, destroying life, order, and form.

The fundamental message of the composite account, as well as both of its Hebrew sources, is theological, not historical. What is presented by the author(s) is a picture of creation corrupted through sin, its original design obscured, its intention betrayed. God responds to this alien development in a manner that suggests not only destruction but also purging, for water—as well as fire—is a common means and symbol of purification in the Old Testament. God's intention in the Flood may be understood, then, as an act of cleansing or purging, so that a new beginning may be made. It is not simply an act of judgment, but the necessary prerequisite for renewal. The account tells us that God treats sin with utmost seriousness. God does not tolerate evil but has the power and will to destroy it. But the Creator and Judge of all the earth is also its savior. God will not cut off all life, but for the sake of one righteous soul will save all. And that is not the end. God's decision to save creation is supported now by a pledge (covenant) to uphold the created order, to stand on the side of life—despite the continuing human inclination to sin. God makes a commitment to the world, to all life, to support it. Through this story of judgment, salvation, and covenant, the author declares that creation is dependent upon God, but also dependable, subject neither to human folly nor divine caprice. Thus the character of God as judge, savior, and sustainer of creation is made known to us at the beginning of the biblical story, and the pattern of God's response to human sin is laid out, a pattern that will be repeated again and again in ever-new forms throughout the biblical story. Historical-critical interpretation helps us to see the essential story within the story, and thus to read it in a way similar to prescientific and precritical reading. But it goes beyond that older reading in enabling us to appreciate the story as heard within its ancient Near Eastern context.

The biblical story of the Deluge did not inform its ancient Hebrew readers of a great flood, for they all knew about that. It was part of the common knowledge of the ancient world. The story had circulated for perhaps a thousand years before the first recorded Hebrew account and existed in a number of different versions. Thus, the biblical writer is using ancient and common lore in recounting the story of the Flood. And that means that the message in the text is to be found primarily in the way the writer *re*tells the story to make his own theological points. Comparison of the biblical version with the Babylonian versions shows some striking differences which point up the message of the Old Testament account. The Flood in the biblical account occurs neither because the gods' sleep is disturbed by the tumult of humans on the earth nor by an apparently arbitrary decision of the divine council, as in the Mesopotamian version, but by the Creator who has observed that the creation has become corrupted by sin, turning away from its maker. The biblical account does not show creation at the mercy of the gods' whims, but under the judgment, and providence, of God. For in the biblical account the destruction is related to the ultimate aim of renewing creation, a renewal accompanied by an eternal covenant. An essential feature of the biblical account is the fact that the Judge and the Savior are one, whereas the savior god of the Babylonian account acts secretly on behalf of his favorite human, divulging the plan of the gods and instructing him on a plan of survival. And the fate of the survivor is also different, for the Baby-

Ionian hero, Utnapishtim, is carried away with his wife to live with the gods, while Noah and his wife become the parents of all the peoples of the earth.

We who know the biblical story know that we are no longer simply the descendants of Adam. We are also the descendants of Noah, children of grace, saved from the waters and given a future secured by God's own commitment. When we read the story of the Flood in its canonical context we must link it to those other stories of judgment and grace, salvation and promise, symbolized by water and covenant: the passage through the sea of the exodus, the baptism of Jesus in the Jordan, the covenants with Abraham and David, and the covenants at Sinai and Shechem and Golgotha. We miss the point if we look for wood from an ancient ark and lose the meaning of the account by attempting to read it as history. Historical-critical scholarship, employed in the context of a church that continues to be guided by its tradition, can guard against the trap of modern mentality by informing us of the symbolic and representational meaning of stories of primordial times; for such stories are always reflections on present realities and never simply accounts of past events. The liturgy of the Easter vigil can be our teacher too. If we have truly understood the biblical flood story, we will respond with a song of thanksgiving that embraces our own story of salvation:

> Like survivors of the Flood,
>   Like walkers through the sea,
>   Like walkers through the God-divided sea:
> We are rescued, we are claimed,
>   we are loved and we are named,
> We are Baptized! I am Baptized!
>   We have passed through the waters
>   And that's all that matters!
> We have passed through the waters!
>   O thanks be to God!
>   (Richard Avery and Donald Marsh)

HISTORICAL CRITICISM AND THE NEW TESTAMENT

Historical criticism helps us to hear the voices of the Bible in conversation with other voices of the environment, voices of the tradition they had received and other voices within the community of Israel or the early Christian movement. It enables us to understand why we have four Gospels instead of one and why they differ as they do. In fact, few of us recognize the differences, since the story of Jesus that we know and the sayings that we remember are a composite of selections from all the Gospels. Our gospel has a birth story with shepherds and wise men, but Luke's Gospel knows no wise men and Matthew's no shepherds, and the Gospels of Mark and John record no birth story at all! The "Seven Last Words" of our Jesus tradition are taken from all four Gospels, and only one (the cry, "My God, my God, why hast thou forsaken me?") occurs in more than a single source (Matthew and Mark). And the well-known Sermon on the Mount is found only in Matthew, while sayings that occur in Matthew's sermon are reported in other contexts in other Gospels. The reason for this diversity within the oldest traditions is that each of the four canonical Gospels represents the gospel as told in and for a particular community in a particular time and place, with particular needs and interests. Each is a selection from the available traditions and each has shaped the tradition in passing it on—not unlike our own selection and shaping.

While scholars continue to debate the details of date, authorship, and place of origin of the Gospels, some distinctive characteristics of each are widely recognized: Matthew's Gospel addresses a Jewish Christian community, probably in Syria, which is deeply concerned with the question of the continuing validity of the Jewish law. Jesus is portrayed for this community as one who fulfills the law and is its true interpreter. The Sermon on the Mount recalls Moses on the mountain. And Jesus is presented as the fulfillment of Old Testament prophecy and Messianic expectations. Matthew introduces Jesus in the genealogy of Abraham and David and repeatedly refers to the Old Testament Scriptures to interpret the life and mission of Christ.

Mark's Gospel, in contrast, addresses a Gentile community, perhaps in Rome. Its poor Greek shows that its author was not well educated or skilled in literary composition. Mark's short Gospel is full of miracles, but its message is directed at those who draw the wrong conclusions from them. Mark insists that the miracles are insufficient evidence of the divinity of Christ and a false sign of authority among believers. It is the passion which Mark stresses as the event that reveals Jesus as the Son of God.

Luke's Gospel is marked by elegant Greek prose, a universalizing emphasis, memorable stories (the prodigal son, the good Samaritan), and a prophetic interest. Its setting appears to be outside of Palestine, in an area where the Jewish Diaspora met the Gentile world. In Luke's portrait, Jesus is the prophet of the last days who confronts Israel with the graciousness of God and breaks down all barriers, even that of Israel. Luke's Jesus announces his mission in words of liberation quoted from the book of Isaiah, and the prophetic note is further sounded in themes of favoritism to the poor and outcasts, emphasis on the role of women, and openness to the Gentiles. In Luke the passion is portrayed as the death of an innocent prophet, while the resurrection is God's "yes" to that prophetic word.

John's Gospel breaks the mold of the other three with a unique style and structure. It contains no parables, but instead offers long speeches in which Jesus instructs his followers. Emphasis is placed on the person of Jesus ("I am . . .") and on his authority as the authority of God. Jesus is presented as the incarnation of the divine Word, which

comes to earth for a time in the earthly ministry of Jesus
and then returns to the Father. The crucifixion, rather
than the resurrection, is the moment of glorification, in
which Jesus is lifted up, signaling his return to his divine
origin. The language and thought of John's Gospel is
shaped by arguments within the Jewish community from
which John's group has separated. It is also heavily influenced by Wisdom speculation and shows affinities with
some Gnostic thought.

In their selection and presentation of the Jesus tradition,
the Gospels contain hints of the conversations and conflicts occurring in the early church, but the letters of Paul
bring that dialogue into the open with pointed pleading,
admonition, denunciation of false teachers and false understandings of the gospel, and justification of his own
teaching. In Paul's letters we see, even more clearly than
in the Gospels, the struggle of the churches to comprehend the new faith and its implications for their lives. May
we eat meat sacrificed to idols? Is circumcision required?
Is the law still binding? On Gentiles? Are sexual relationships compatible with membership in the body of Christ?
Are we not free to do as the Spirit moves us? What are the
signs of the new morality? If we allow ourselves to stand
with Paul and those he addresses, we will recognize that
the same struggle to comprehend the meaning of the gospel and live according to it is ours as well. In that effort,
past and present, the tradition provides the primary
guide, but it is never alone sufficient, for its voices are
many, its occasions different from ours, and its thought
never completely our own, however much we cherish it.
So we must continue the work which the Scriptures have
begun and for which they train us, telling the old story in
a new day and drawing out its implications for our lives.

The Gospels, the letters of Paul, and the other New
Testament writings have one compound question at their

heart: Who is this Jesus; and what difference does it make?
The answers are drawn from the Jewish Scriptures and
from the religious and philosophical thought of the day,
interacting with the church's memory of Jesus and its continuing experience of the risen Christ. Who is this Jesus?
A new Moses, teacher and interpreter of the law; Elijah
returned, the prophet of the end time who announces the
advent of God's reign; the "Son of Man" who comes with
the clouds to judge the world on the final day; the Messiah,
who will deliver and restore Israel; king of the Jews—of
royal lineage, born in the city of David, paid homage by
the kings of the Gentiles, . . . crucified (what kind of king
is this?); the suffering servant of God; the sacrificial lamb
that atones for sin; a great high priest of the order of
Melchizedek; the preexistent Logos; divine Wisdom; the
Son of God; Lord; Immanuel: God with us. All of these
answers, which the New Testament offers from its Old
Testament heritage and the wisdom of its day, interpret
Christ for us, and from them and the wisdom of our day
we must continue the work of interpreting Christ.

CONCLUSION: WORD AND PRESENCE

We have received the Bible as the word of God, but
often we hear only human voices and turn away in disap-
pointment. We look for a clear and constant word and find
instead a babel of sounds. We seek a simple message and
refuse to believe it when it is given. For the word of God
which echoes through the Scriptures from beginning to
end—and beyond—is always the same and always new: "I
am with you, and I will be with you always." That is the
message revealed to Moses in the divine name, the word
of assurance spoken to the prophet Jeremiah at his call, the
promise of Immanuel, and the meaning of the incarnation
and the resurrection. From the days of our expulsion from

the Garden and the subsiding of the Flood to the day of
Pentecost that has been the constant message: God with
us—from the beginning to the end.

But we have always wanted more: a vision, an experience, a formula, that will dispel uncertainty forever and
remove the need for judgment and decision—and faith.
We are like Moses on the mountain, who has just spent
forty days and forty nights alone with God; but when God
tells him to move on, to set out on an unknown way, all
that he has seen and heard is forgotten. "You have not let
me know whom you will send with me," Moses says, and
God replies, "My presence will go with you." But Moses
continues to press for further assurances, until at last he
comes to his final plea: "Show me your glory!" which is to
say: Show me your unmediated presence, your face. And
God in gracious condescension passes before him, cover-
ing him with a protecting hand, and revealing at last the
back, but not the face (Exodus 33).

That is what the Bible does for us. It allows us to see God
passing, in a view from behind. It shows us where God has
been and what God has done, as seen and experienced by
our biblical ancestors. It shows us God's presence with
them, leading them through the waters and through the
unknown wilderness. But it is always a view from behind.
For at the moment that the One who has accompanied
them is recognized, when they would gaze into God's face
or reach out and touch, the face is turned and the presence
withdrawn. So it was in the appearances of God to
Abraham and Gideon and the mother of Samson; at the
moment of recognition the divine visitor was gone, leaving only the memory imprinted on the heart and mind.

But surely that has changed in Christ, for the New Testament assures us that the God whom none has ever seen
has been made manifest at last in a Son. That is the testimony of John, who declares that he "dwelt among us

... [and] we have beheld his glory" (John 1:14). But that is the testimony of faith; it is the sight given to the blind. For when Jesus was among us, those who knew him best did not recognize whom they had seen. The Gospel writer proclaimed his birth as the fulfillment of the prophecy of Immanuel: God with us (Matt. 1:23); but those to whom he came said, "Isn't this the carpenter, Mary's son . . . and aren't his sisters here with us?" (Mark 6:3). He healed the sick, restored sight to the blind, fed the hungry and cast out demons, and they said he was a madman, possessed by the lord of demons, and they demanded that he be crucified—and everyone deserted him, even his disciples.

But that was not the end. On the road to Emmaus and at the evening meal, on other roads and at other meals, the stranger who has accompanied us is made known. But at the moment that we would hold him he is gone. If we would know him, we must continue on the journey and in the fellowship of the meal. Two things are necessary for the knowledge we seek. One is knowledge of the Scriptures, for it is there that the signs are given in the testimony of those who have preceded us. It is there that the story is found which the Stranger opened to the disciples on the road. The other is the fellowship of the disciples, or the church, for that is the context in which recognition occurs, where word and presence come together in the breaking of bread. The experience of recognition is for those who have lived with Christ and shared the hope and agony of his ministry, his last days, and the covenant meal. For those who have not shared those hopes and disappointments there is no recognition, only words and ritual.

The Scriptures are not the word of God and they do not contain the word of God. They are the place where the church hears God speaking and discerns God's presence when their words are studied and pondered and questioned—and opened for us by the Stranger who accompanies us on our journey and breaks bread with us. When that occurs, we respond rightly with the words of the liturgy:

> This is the word of the Lord.
> *Thanks be to God!*

QUESTIONS FOR DISCUSSION

Chapter 1. THE NEW COMMUNITY IN CHRIST

1. The New Testament makes clear connections between church life (baptismal practices, celebration of the Lord's Supper, etc.) and the shape of community life. What connections can you see in your tradition? If connections are not obvious, why is that the case?

2. Baptism in particular has become a controversial topic in Protestant churches in the last decade. What images does the baptismal service provide for picturing the life of faith? What do you make of the baptismal imagery in Paul's letters and the way Paul uses the imagery?

3. Paul's letter to the church at Corinth seeks to help Christians learn to live together even when they do not agree about everything. In what ways does your tradition seek to nurture life together while leaving open areas of legitimate disagreement?

4. Paul's congregations provided radical social alternatives in a world that defined human life in terms of rigid economic, racial, and sexual categories. To what extent do our congregations still offer such alternatives? If things have changed, why?

5. What might be considered a legitimate range of options for Christians with regard to such controversial issues

when was it completed? Does it contain all of the books used as Scripture in the early church? What factors influenced the final selection?

5. What does it mean to speak of the "canon" or "canonical Scriptures"?

Chapter 3. SOLA SCRIPTURA

1. What were the main ways of interpreting Scripture in the early church and in the Middle Ages?

2. What were the problems of a literal reading? of allegorical interpretation? What was the "rule of faith"?

3. What is the meaning of *"sola scriptura"*?

4. Why did Luther stress the "plain" or "literal" meaning of the text and what did he mean by these expressions? What were the consequences of this emphasis?

5. How did Calvin understand the inspiration of Scripture?

6. How was Protestant worship affected by the Reformers' understanding of Scripture?

7. How were traditional views of the Bible and traditional ways of interpreting it affected by the Renaissance and the Enlightenment?

8. Why did the new study of the Bible focus on the question of sources and authorship of the biblical books? Why did this study appear to undermine the Bible's authority?

Chapter 4. THE NEW CRITICISM

1. Why was the new biblical scholarship of the seventeenth and eighteenth centuries felt as a threat by most of the church at the time? What were the consequences of the early opposition for the development of biblical scholarship and its relation to the church?

2. Why did biblical scholarship play such a small role in American religion until the end of the nineteenth century?

3. Why were the scientific theories of Darwin considered a threat to biblical faith? How did historical-critical understanding of the Bible help the church in England to resolve the controversy? Why is there still a controversy in America?

4. How did liberals and conservatives differ in their understandings of the Bible and of biblical authority?

5. What did Hodge and Warfield understand by the inerrancy of Scripture? Why did Briggs view the doctrine as an attempt to "prop up divine authority by human authority"?

6. How did the battles over the Bible at the beginning of this century affect your denomination? To what extent is the argument over appropriate or inappropriate methods of interpreting Scripture an issue in your church today (locally or nationally)?

Chapter 5. INCARNATE WORD

1. In what sense is the word of God in the Bible an "incarnate" word?

2. Why is reading the Bible like a journey to a foreign land? How can the Bible be the word of God for all people?

3. In what sense is the Bible story? Israel's story? God's story? Our story?

4. What are the primary questions that underlie the Bible's testimony? To what extent are they the same as or different from ours today? How can biblical answers to problems of another time become appropriate to our own time?

5. Why does the church need the whole Bible? What would be the result if we passed on to the next generation

only those portions of the Bible that we understood or approved?

6. In what sense is the Bible "overheard" speech?

Chapter 6. "ABRAHAM BEGAT ISAAC"

1. What parts of the Bible or what things about the Bible have been a "stone" for you? Where have you found "bread" in the Bible?

2. What are your favorite biblical books or passages? Why do you like them? What could you say to someone who disagreed with things read in the Bible?

3. What Bible aids have you found most useful? What translation (version) of the Bible do you like best? Why?

4. How do the genealogies of Jesus in Matthew and Luke differ? What is the theological significance of the differences?

5. In what ways has the Bible been considered "sexist"? How does this affect its message for us?

Chapter 7. THE STRANGER ON THE ROAD:
HISTORICAL CRITICISM
AND THE CHURCH'S FAITH

1. What is the difference between the historical approaches of "fundamentalist" and "critical" scholars? In what sense can critical scholars be said to be more "literal" in their reading than fundamentalists?

2. What is the aim of historical-critical interpretation of Scripture? In what sense is it an incomplete method?

3. What "new twist" is given to the Flood story when it is read in the context of other ancient flood stories? In what ways are the liturgical understanding of the Flood story and the historical-critical understanding similar?

4. What are some examples of the differences among the Gospels and what do they tell us about the way the gospel

was heard and related in the communities for which they were written?

5. To what extent does one's understanding of the Bible today depend on the sharing of the life and faith of a community?

6. In what sense does the Bible give us a view of God "from behind"?

7. In what sense is the Bible the word of God?

FOR FURTHER READING / REFERENCES

Chapter 1. THE CHURCH'S BOOK

Paul J. Achtemeier. *The Inspiration of Scripture: Problems and Proposals.* Westminster Press, 1980.
Bruce C. Birch and Larry L. Rasmussen. *Bible and Ethics in the Christian Life.* Augsburg Publishing House, 1976.
Victor P. Furnish. *The Moral Teaching of Paul.* Abingdon Press, 1979.
David H. Kelsey. *The Uses of Scripture in Recent Theology.* Fortress Press, 1975.

Works Used in This Chapter

The Worshipbook (Presbyterian; 1970); *The Book of Common Prayer* (Episcopal; 1977); *People's Mass Book* (Roman Catholic; 1970); *Services of the Church* (United Church of Christ; 1969); *Lutheran Book of Worship* (1978); *The Book of Worship* (Methodist; 1965); Peter D. Day, *Eastern Liturgies* (Irish University Press, 1972); Bard Thompson, ed., *Liturgies of the Western Church* (World Publishing Company, 1961; Luther excerpt from p. 129; quoted from *Works of Martin Luther,* Vol. VI [Muhlenberg Press, 1932], pp. 170ff.); Massey H. Shepherd, Jr., *The*

Oxford American Prayer Book Commentary (Oxford University Press, 1950); and Emory Stevens Bucke, ed., *Companion to the Hymnal* (Abingdon Press, 1970).

Chapter 2. CRISIS AND CANON

Grant, Robert M. *A Short History of the Interpretation of the Bible.* Macmillan Co., 1963.

Works Used in This Chapter

Hans von Campenhausen, *The Formation of the Christian Bible* (tr. by J. A. Baker; Fortress Press, 1972, 1977; quotations from pp. 74 and 167); *The Cambridge History of the Bible*, Vol. 1, *From the Beginnings to Jerome*, ed. by P. R. Ackroyd and C. F. Evans (Cambridge University Press, 1970); John H. Hayes, *An Introduction to Old Testament Study* (Abingdon Press, 1979); and Richard N. Soulen, *Handbook of Biblical Criticism* (John Knox Press, 1976).

Chapter 3. SOLA SCRIPTURA

Hans W. Frei. *The Eclipse of Biblical Narrative: A Study in 18th and 19th Century Hermeneutics.* Yale University Press, 1974.

Works Used in This Chapter

Frei (quotation from p. 3); Peter Stuhlmacher, *Historical Criticism and Theological Interpretation of Scripture* (tr. by Roy A. Harrisville; Fortress Press, 1977; quotation of Augustine from p. 20); Hayes, *An Introduction to Old Testament Study* (quotation of Luther from p. 103); *The Cambridge History of the Bible*, Vol. 3, *The West from the Reformation to the Present Day*, ed. by S. L. Greenslade

(Cambridge University Press, 1963); J. K. S. Reid, *The Authority of Scripture: A Study of the Reformation and Post-Reformation Understanding of the Bible* (Harper & Brothers, 1957; quotation of Luther from p. 70); Thompson, *Liturgies of the Western Church* (quotation of Luther from p. 132); and Shepherd, *The Oxford American Prayer Book Commentary.*

Chapter 4. THE NEW CRITICISM

George A. Buttrick, ed. *The Interpreter's Dictionary of the Bible*, Vol. I. Abingdon Press, 1962: "Biblical Criticism, History of," pp. 413–418.

Stephen C. Neill. *The Interpretation of the New Testament, 1861–1961.* Oxford University Press, 1964.

Lloyd R. Bailey. *The Pentateuch* (Interpreting Biblical Texts). Abingdon Press, 1981.

Jerry Wayne Brown. *The Rise of Biblical Criticism in America 1800–1870: The New England Scholars.* Wesleyan University Press, 1969.

Works Used in This Chapter

The Cambridge History of the Bible, Vol. 3; Sydney E. Ahlstrom, *A Religious History of the American People* (Yale University Press, 1972); and H. Shelton Smith, Robert T. Handy, and Lefferts A. Loetscher, *American Christianity: An Historical Interpretation with Representative Documents*, 2 vols. (Charles Scribner's Sons, 1960, 1963; quotations of Hodge and Warfield from Vol. II, p. 332, and Briggs from Vol. II, p. 276).

Chapter 5. INCARNATE WORD

Dennis Nineham, *The Use and Abuse of the Bible.* Harper & Row, Barnes & Noble Book, 1976.

James Barr. *The Scope and Authority of the Bible.* Westminster Press, 1980.

Hans Küng and Jürgen Moltmann, eds. *Conflicting Ways of Interpreting the Bible (Concilium).* Seabury Press, 1980.

Jack B. Rogers and Donald K. McKim. *The Authority and Interpretation of the Bible: An Historical Approach.* Harper & Row, 1979.

Chapter 6. "Abraham Begat Isaac"

Walter Brueggemann. *The Bible Makes Sense.* John Knox Press, 1977.

H. W. Wolff. *The Old Testament: A Guide to Its Writings,* tr. by Keith R. Crim. Fortress Press, 1973.

Günther Bornkamm. *The New Testament: A Guide to Its Writings,* tr. by Reginald H. Fuller and Ilse Fuller. Fortress Press, 1973.

Works Used in This Chapter

Achtemeier, *The Inspiration of Scripture,* especially p. 95; *The Interpreter's Dictionary of the Bible,* Vol. II: "Genealogy" and "Genealogy (Christ)," pp. 362–366; and Supplementary Volume: "Genealogy (Christ)," p. 354.

Chapter 7. The Stranger on the Road: Historical Criticism and the Church's Faith

Lloyd R. Bailey. *Where Is Noah's Ark?* Abingdon Press, Festival Books, 1978.